Where do I go for answers to my travel questions?

What's the best and easiest way to plan and book my trip?

frommers.travelocity.com

Frommer's, the travel guide leader, has teamed up with **Travelocity.com**, the leader in online travel, to bring you an in-depth, easy-to-use resource designed to help you plan and book your trip online.

At **frommers.travelocity.com**, you'll find free online updates about your destination from the experts at Frommer's plus the outstanding travel planning and purchasing features of Travelocity.com. Travelocity.com provides reservations capabilities for 95 percent of all airline seats sold, more than 47,000 hotels, and over 50 car rental companies. In addition, Travelocity.com offers more than 2,000 exciting vacation and cruise packages. Travelocity.com puts you in complete control of your travel planning with these and other great features:

> **Expert travel guidance from Frommer's** - over 150 writers reporting from around the world!
>
> **Best Fare Finder** - an interactive calendar tells you when to travel to get the best airfare
>
> **Fare Watcher** - we'll track airfare changes to your favorite destinations
>
> **Dream Maps** - a mapping feature that suggests travel opportunities based on your budget
>
> **Shop Safe Guarantee** - 24 hours a day / 7 days a week live customer service, and more!

Whether traveling on a tight budget, looking for a quick weekend getaway, or planning the trip of a lifetime, Frommer's guides and Travelocity.com will make your travel dreams a reality. You've bought the book, now book the trip!

Travelocity.com
A Sabre Company

Frommer's®

A New Star-Rating System & Other Exciting News from Frommer's!

In our continuing effort to publish the savviest, most up-to-date, and most appealing travel guides available, we've added some great new features.

Frommer's guides now include a new **star-rating system.** Every hotel, restaurant, and attraction is rated from 0 to 3 stars to help you set priorities and organize your time.

We've also added **seven brand-new features** that point you to the great deals, in-the-know advice, and unique experiences that separate travelers from tourists. Throughout the guide look for:

Finds	Special finds—those places only insiders know about
Fun Fact	Fun facts—details that make travelers more informed and their trips more fun
Kids	Best bets for kids—advice for the whole family
Moments	Special moments—those experiences that memories are made of
Overrated	Places or experiences not worth your time or money
Tips	Insider tips—some great ways to save time and money
Value	Great values—where to get the best deals

Zion & Bryce Canyon National Parks

3rd Edition

by Don & Barbara Laine

Hungry Minds™

Best-Selling Books • Digital Downloads • e-Books
Answer Networks • e-Newsletters • Branded Web Sites • e-Learning
New York, NY • Cleveland, OH • Indianapolis, IN

ABOUT THE AUTHORS

Residents of northern New Mexico for more than 30 years, **Don** and **Barbara Laine** have traveled extensively throughout the Rocky Mountains and the Southwest. They are the authors of *Frommer's Colorado, Frommer's Rocky Mountain National Park, Frommer's Yosemite and Sequoia/Kings Canyon National Parks,* and *Frommer's Utah;* are the lead authors of *Frommer's National Parks of the American West;* and have contributed to *Frommer's Texas* and *Frommer's USA.* The Laines have also written *Little-Known Southwest* and *New Mexico & Arizona State Parks* (both for The Mountaineers Books).

Published by:

HUNGRY MINDS, INC.

909 Third Ave.
New York, NY 10022

ISBN 0-7645-6559-1
ISSN 1093-9806

Editor: Christine Ryan
Production Editor: Tammy Ahrens
Photo Editor: Richard Fox
Cartographer: Roberta Stockwell
Production by Hungry Minds Indianapolis Production Services

Illustrations on p. 152 (Douglas Fir), 159 (Coyote), 160, 161 (Mule Deer), 162 (Pronghorn), 164 (American Dipper, Bald Eagle, Golden Eagle), 165 and 168 (Red-Tailed Hawk) by Jasper Burna; illustrations on p. 151, 152 (Juniper), 153, 154, 155, 156, 159 (Chipmunk), 161 (Mountain Lion), 162 (Prairie Dog, Black-Tailed Jackrabbit, Desert Cottontail), 163, 164 (Mountain Chickadee), 166, 167, 168 (Peregrine Falcon), 169, 170, and 171 by Giselle Simons.

SPECIAL SALES

For general information on Hungry Minds' products and services, please contact our Customer Care department; within the U.S. at 800-762-2974, outside the U.S. at 317-572-3993 or fax 317-572-4002. For sales inquiries and reseller information, including discounts, bulk sales, customized editions, and premium sales, please contact our Customer Care department at 800-434-3422.

Manufactured in the United States of America

5 4 3 2 1

Contents

List of Maps

ACKNOWLEDGMENTS

The authors are very grateful for the help of Ron Terry at Zion National Park, Cheryl Schreier at Bryce Canyon National Park, and Steve Robinson at Cedar Breaks National Monument.

AN INVITATION TO THE READER

In researching this book, we discovered many wonderful places—hotels, restaurants, shops, and more. We're sure you'll find others. Please tell us about them, so we can share the information with your fellow travelers in upcoming editions. If you were disappointed with a recommendation, we'd love to know that, too. Please write to:

Frommer's Zion & Bryce Canyon National Parks, 3rd Edition
Hungry Minds, Inc. • 909 Third Avenue • New York, NY 10022

AN ADDITIONAL NOTE

Please be advised that travel information is subject to change at any time—and this is especially true of prices. We therefore suggest that you write or call ahead for confirmation when making your travel plans. The authors, editors, and publisher cannot be held responsible for the experiences of readers while traveling. Your safety is important to us, however, so we encourage you to stay alert and be aware of your surroundings. Keep a close eye on cameras, purses, and wallets, all favorite targets of thieves and pickpockets.

WHAT THE SYMBOLS MEAN

The following abbreviations are used for credit cards:

AE	American Express	DISC	Discover	V	Visa
DC	Diners Club	MC	MasterCard		

FROMMERS.COM

Now that you have the guidebook to a great trip, visit our website at **www.frommers.com** for travel information on nearly 2,000 destinations. With features updated regularly, we give you instant access to the most current trip-planning information available. At Frommers.com, you'll also find the best prices on airfares, accommodations, and car rentals—and you can even book travel online through our travel booking partners. At Frommers.com, you'll also find the following:

- Daily Newsletter highlighting the best travel deals
- Hot Spot of the Month/Vacation Sweepstakes & Travel Photo Contest
- More than 200 Travel Message Boards
- Outspoken Newsletters and Feature Articles on travel bargains, vacation ideas, tips & resources, and more!

Here's what the critics say about Frommer's:

"The only mainstream guide to list specific prices. The Walter Cronkite of guidebooks—with all that implies."

—*Travel & Leisure*

"Complete, concise, and filled with useful information."

—*New York Daily News*

"Amazingly easy to use. Very portable, very complete."

—*Booklist*

"Hotel Information is close to encylopedic."

—*Des Moines Sunday Register*

"Detailed, accurate and easy-to-read information for all price ranges."

—*Glamour Magazine*

Introducing Zion & Bryce Canyon National Parks

There aren't many places in the world where the forces of nature have come together with such dramatic results as in Zion and Bryce Canyon National Parks. From arid desert and desolate canyons, to pine-covered peaks and awe-inspiring rock formations, these two parks—located about 85 miles apart in colorful southern Utah—offer some of the American West's most beautiful scenery, along with almost unlimited opportunities for hiking, camping, and other outdoor experiences.

Zion and Bryce Canyon sit on the vast, high Colorado Plateau. They share this plateau with Utah's three other national parks (Arches, Canyonlands, and Capitol Reef), as well as with Grand Canyon National Park in Arizona, Mesa Verde National Park in Colorado, Chaco Culture National Historical Park in New Mexico, a number of national monuments and state parks, the Hopi Indian reservation, and the vast Navajo Nation, home of America's largest Indian tribe.

The Colorado Plateau developed millions of years ago when forces deep within the earth forced the crust to rise, exposing many strata of rocks. Over several million more years, the power of erosion and weathering sculpted spectacular rock formations, colored with an iron-rich palette of reds, oranges, pinks, and browns.

Both Zion and Bryce Canyon National Parks are known for their stunning rock formations—Zion for its massive sandstone monoliths, and Bryce for its more delicate limestone sculptures. But the wondrous natural architecture isn't the sole reason for visiting these parks. You will also find shimmering pools of deep green water, a sometimes-roaring river, forests of pine and fir, broad panoramic views, a vast array of plants and animals, and even a bit of human history, all of which are discussed in the following pages.

Butch Cassidy Slept Here

Robert LeRoy Parker was born into a Mormon family in Beaver, Utah on April 13, 1866. The oldest of 13 children, Robert worked on the small ranch his parents bought near Circleville, about 50 miles north of Bryce Canyon.

It was in Circleville where the problems began, when the teenager fell in with some unsavory characters, including Mike Cassidy, who gave the youth his first gun and eventually his last name. Setting out to make his mark in the world, the boy eventually made his way to Telluride, Colorado, where strangely enough the Telluride bank was robbed. Butch Cassidy had officially begun his life of crime.

In the following years, Butch—who gained the nickname after a short stint working in a butcher shop—became expert at rustling cattle, robbing banks, and finally his ultimate glory, robbing trains. Often he and his gang would travel through Utah, hiding out in the desolate badlands, including, it's believed, what is now Bryce Canyon National Park. Butch's gang raised such hell that saloon keepers began calling them "that wild bunch," and the name stuck.

Those who have seen the 1969 movie *Butch Cassidy and the Sundance Kid*, with Paul Newman as Butch and Robert Redford as his partner-in-crime Sundance, will recall the spectacular scene in which Butch and his cohorts use too much dynamite to open a safe in a railroad car. Apparently it's basically true and took place on June 2, 1899, near Wilcox, Wyoming. According to reports of the day, they got away with $30,000.

The Union Pacific Railroad took exception to Butch's antics, and when the posses started getting a bit too close, Butch, Sundance, and Sundance's lady friend Etta Place took off for South America, where it is said they continued a life of crime for a half-dozen or so years.

Then, according to some historians and the movie version of Butch's life, Butch and Sundance were shot dead in a gun battle with army troops in Bolivia. Some, though, believe otherwise—that Butch returned to the United States, visited friends and family in Utah and Wyoming, and eventually settled in Spokane, Washington, where he lived a peaceful and respectable life under the name William T. Phillips, dying of natural causes in 1937.

Southwestern Utah

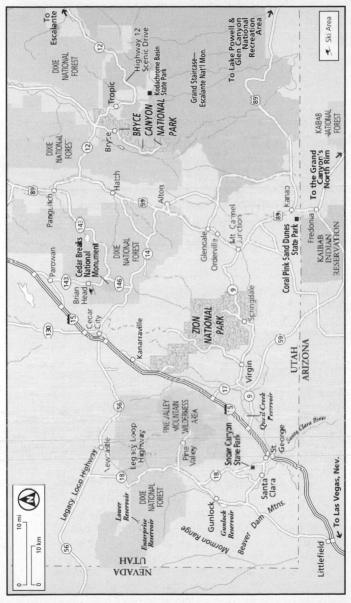

One thing that makes both parks so inviting is that they can be experienced in a variety of ways. Adventurers can savor challenging hiking trails and backcountry routes, while the simply curious can examine millions of years of geologic history and have the chance to see rare plants and animals. Meanwhile, those with an artistic bent can simply lose themselves in the beauty of the parks.

In searching for the essence of these natural worlds, you'll find well-developed and maintained trail systems, overlooks offering panoramic vistas, interpretative displays, museum programs, and knowledgeable park rangers ready to help you make the most of your visit. You can't possibly see everything there is to be seen here, and you shouldn't try. Zion and Bryce Canyon are not to be visited as if they were amusement parks, racing from ride to ride; these natural wonders are to be savored, embraced, and explored, and the best way to do that is to slow down. Take time to ponder the sunrise, sit quietly at the edge of a meadow and wait for a deer to emerge from the woods, and even, as the cliché goes, stop and smell the roses.

It's certain that you won't see every corner of these two parks even on a long vacation of 2 or 3 weeks. Bryce Amphitheater is enormous, filled with countless delightfully shaped and colored formations and groups of formations, with telling names such as Wall Street, Fairyland Canyon, and Queen's Garden. Meanwhile, the rugged stone monuments at Zion, such as the Watchman and the West Temple, are overpowering and tend to underline the insignificance of mankind in the total scheme of things. But among America's western parks, these are two of the easiest to explore, to feel that you've gotten to know their very being. In large part this is because their extensive trail and road systems enable the visitor to explore these parks in fairly small, easily digestible bites, sampling one aspect, letting it settle, and then moving along for another taste.

Bryce Canyon National Park is a bit more user-friendly than Zion, while Zion offers a greater variety of experiences, from river canyons with colorful gardens to rocky windswept ridges. Bryce also has several fairly easy trails that lead right into the middle of some of its best scenery. This isn't to say that Zion is hard to get into, but because of the greater variety of terrain it takes a bit more time and effort to achieve that same feeling that you *know* the park.

One interesting difference between the parks is that at Zion the visitor arrives at the bottom of the canyon, and in most cases looks and hikes up toward the rock formations. At Bryce Canyon you arrive at the top, along the rim, and look and then hike down into the amphitheaters. Foot-power is the best way to explore both parks, although those without the physical ability or desire to hike find that there is quite a bit for them to see, as well. Zion has the greatest variety of hiking trails—more than double the number at Bryce—as well as more extreme variations in elevation and terrain. Because Zion is lower, you'll find more favorable hiking conditions in winter there, while summer hikers will appreciate the cooler temperatures in the higher elevations of Bryce Canyon.

1 The Best of Zion & Bryce Canyon National Parks

From their rocky trails to their deep forests, Zion and Bryce Canyon National Parks are enchanting worlds of discovery, spectacular scenic wonders, and magnificent outdoor playgrounds. In fact, the only real problems are choosing what to do, what to see, where to stay, and even where to eat. Because it can be bewildering to try to plan your trip with so many options, we've assembled the very best that these parks and the surrounding areas have to offer.

THE BEST DAY HIKES

- **Emerald Pools Trail System** (Zion National Park): If green is your color, you'll love this trail—algae keeps the three pools glowing a deep, rich, and yes, emerald green. The first part of the trail leads through a forest to the Lower Emerald Pool, with its lovely waterfall and hanging garden. See chapter 4.
- **East Mesa Trail** (Zion National Park): Allow a full day for this 6-mile hike, which is an easier and shorter route to Observation Point than the Observation Point Trail. From the promontory you'll get spectacular views down Zion Canyon, with the Great White Throne in the foreground and Red Arch Mountain beyond. See chapter 4.
- **Navajo Loop/Queen's Garden Trail** (Bryce Canyon National Park): To truly experience magical Bryce Canyon, you should hike down into it, and this not-too-difficult combination trail is the perfect way to go. Start at Sunset Point and get the steepest part out of the way first. You'll see Thor's Hammer, the towering skyscrapers of Wall Street, and some of the park's most fanciful formations, including majestic Queen Victoria. See chapter 7.
- **Rim Trail** (Bryce Canyon National Park): This underrated trail is a delight, providing splendid views down into spectacularly

scenic Bryce Amphitheater from a variety of vantage points over its 5½-mile length. More walking than hiking, the Rim Trail includes a half-mile section between two overlooks—Sunrise and Sunset—that is suitable for wheelchairs. Views are especially fine early in the morning, when you can watch the changing light on the red rocks below. See chapter 7.

THE BEST BACKCOUNTRY HIKES

- **Hiking the Narrows** (Zion National Park): This is an experience unique to Zion National Park—a 1,000-foot-deep canyon, with water filling it from side to side in most places. Although much of Zion is dry rock, this is anything but, and it's an incredible experience for those in good shape and with strong nerves. It can be experienced in three ways—as a short day hike, full-day hike, or an overnight hike—but all involve getting wet. *Warning:* Because the Narrows is prone to flash flooding, check weather forecasts carefully before setting out. See chapter 4.

- **Riggs Spring Loop Trail** (Bryce Canyon National Park): Although this 9-mile loop can be hiked in 1 day, it's better as an overnight backpacking trip. This enables you to take your time to see wildlife (possibly even a mountain lion), as you hike through forests of Douglas fir, ponderosa pines, piñons, and aspen, with views of the white and pink cliffs soaring above. See chapter 7.

THE BEST WILDLIFE VIEWING SPOTS

- **Hiking the Angels Landing Trail** (Zion National Park): This difficult hike provides opportunities to see mule deer, golden eagles, peregrine falcons, and lizards; it also offers splendid views into Zion Canyon. *Warning:* The last half mile of this trail is along a knife-edge ridge—*definitely* not for anyone with a fear of heights. See chapters 4 and 10.

- **The Riverside Walk** (Zion National Park): Here, deep in a slot canyon carved by the Virgin River, you're apt to see the American dipper—also called the water ouzel—as it dives into the water in search of aquatic insects. This is also the only place in the world where you'll find the Zion snail, although it may be hard to recognize, since it is only ⅛ inch across. *Warning:* Because the Narrows is prone to flash flooding, check weather forecasts carefully before setting out. See chapters 4 and 10.

- **Weeping Rock Area** (Zion National Park): Easily accessible via a short but steep paved trail, Weeping Rock oozes water that nurtures lush hanging gardens and produces the perfect habitat for a variety of wildlife, especially birds. Watch for peregrine falcons, American dippers, canyon wrens, and white-throated swifts. See chapters 4 and 10.
- **Riggs Spring Loop Trail** (Bryce Canyon National Park): This little-used backcountry trail through a woodland provides an opportunity to see a variety of wildlife, possibly even one of the park's elusive mountain lions. See chapters 7 and 10.
- **Campgrounds** (both Zion and Bryce Canyon National Parks): It couldn't be easier to see wildlife. Simply sit quietly at your campsite, preferably when few people are in the campground, and wait. You'll see Uinta chipmunks in both parks, white-tailed antelope squirrels at Zion, and golden-mantled ground squirrels at Bryce Canyon. There are almost always plenty of birds, and you're also apt to see mule deer, especially in Watchman Campground at Zion National Park. See chapters 5, 8, and 10.

THE BEST SCENIC VIEWS

- **Zion Canyon Scenic Drive** (Zion National Park): The 14-mile drive through Zion Canyon is impressive no matter how you do it—in your own vehicle (in winter only) or on the shuttle from spring through fall. In every direction the views are awe-inspiring, as the massive stone formations reach for the heavens. The road also provides easy access to a number of wonderful viewpoints and trail heads just off the roadway. See chapter 3.
- **Angels Landing Trail** (Zion National Park): The strenuous Angels Landing Trail leads across a high narrow ridge to a spectacular and dizzying view of Zion Canyon. *Warning:* The last half mile of this trail is along a knife-edge ridge—*definitely* not for anyone with a fear of heights. See chapters 3 and 4.
- **The Narrows** (Zion National Park): The sheer 1,000-foot-high walls are awe-inspiring, almost frightening, as they enclose you in a narrow world of hanging gardens, waterfalls, and sculpted sandstone arches, with the Virgin River pouring over and around your feet and legs. The Narrows are too narrow to allow you to walk next to the river, so you have to wade right through it—but the views make it worth getting wet. *Warning:* Because

the Narrows is prone to flash flooding, check weather forecasts carefully before setting out. See chapter 3 and 4.

- **Inspiration Point** (Bryce Canyon National Park): An appropriately named stop, Inspiration Point provides a phenomenal view down into Bryce Amphitheater, the park's largest and most colorful natural amphitheater. From here you see the Silent City, packed with hoodoos (rock formations) and inspiring to the imagination. Some claim the view is even better just south of Inspiration Point along the Rim Trail, up a little rise, at what is usually called Upper Inspiration Point. See chapters 6 and 7.

- **The Queen's Garden Trail** (Bryce Canyon National Park): Presided over by majestic Queen Victoria, these thousands of colorful and intricately sculpted spires present a magnificent display when viewed from the rim. From the trail below, they're even better. See chapters 6 and 7.

- **The Rim at Sunrise** (Bryce Canyon National Park): If you thought the hoodoos were magnificent in the full light of day, wait until you see them reflecting the deep colors of the morning sun as it rises slowly above the rim. The changing angle of light creates a constantly moving panorama of shadow and color. Walk along the Rim Trail or stop at the viewpoints along the northern half of the park's scenic drive. See chapters 6 and 7.

THE BEST NATURAL SPECTACLES

- **The Great White Throne** (Zion National Park): A huge white monolith, the Great White Throne demands attention no matter when you first glimpse it. Considered the symbol of Zion National Park, this massive block of Navajo sandstone towers is 2,000 feet high, and can be seen from the scenic drive as well as from several hiking trails, including Observation Point Trail, Deertrap Mountain Trail, Angels Landing Trail, and Emerald Pools Trail. See chapters 3 and 4.

- **The Narrows** (Zion National Park): It's difficult to comprehend that this beautiful canyon, 1,000 feet deep and less than 30 feet wide in places, was carved from solid stone, beginning millions of years ago, by the often gently flowing Virgin River at your feet. But to see the flip side of the river, just wait for a rainstorm; it becomes an angry, destructive force that you can well imagine would slice through anything that got in its way. *Warning:* Because the Narrows is prone to flash flooding, check weather forecasts carefully before setting out. See chapters 3 and 4.

- **Queen Victoria** (Bryce Canyon National Park): Among the most impressive hoodoos in the park, from the right angle this honestly looks just like the photos of England's Queen Victoria you see in books and magazines. It even has the same air of superiority. See chapter 7.

- **Bryce Amphitheater Capped with Snow** (Bryce Canyon National Park): The hoodoos become transformed into intricately carved creatures topped with white icing, a fairyland in orange and white. You'll get great views either from stops along the scenic drive or by walking the Rim Trail. See chapters 6 and 7.

THE BEST WINTER SPORTS LOCATION

- **Fairyland Loop Trail** (Bryce Canyon National Park): There aren't many cross country ski trails that can match Bryce Canyon's Fairyland Loop for scenic beauty. The trail leads 1 mile through a pine and juniper forest to the Fairyland Point Overlook, with its spectacular views into Bryce Amphitheater, where a blanket of snow adorns the multicolored hoodoos with a sparkling white mantle. See chapters 6 and 7.

THE BEST HISTORIC SITE

- **Bryce Canyon Lodge** (Bryce Canyon National Park): Built by the Union Pacific Railroad and opened in 1924, this handsome sandstone and ponderosa pine lodge with its large stone fireplace in the lobby has been faithfully restored to its 1920s appearance. The lobby contains historic photos taken in the park during that period. See chapter 8.

THE BEST CHILDREN'S & FAMILY EXPERIENCES

- **Junior Rangers Program** (Zion National Park): Although Junior Ranger programs are available at most national parks, the one offered at Zion each summer is quite extensive, with both morning and afternoon activities that teach kids what makes this natural wonder so special. See chapter 3.

- **Weeping Rock Trail** (Zion National Park): This short hike on a paved trail has interpretive signs explaining the natural history of the area. But the best part is at the end, when the trail arrives at a rock alcove with lush hanging gardens of ferns and wildflowers, where you can lift your face to receive a cooling spray of mist from above. See chapter 4.

- **Queen's Garden Trail** (Bryce Canyon National Park): Not only is this trail fairly easy, but it drops down into one of the most scenic parts of the park, meandering among unique and oddly carved hoodoos. It's fun to let your imagination run wild, both for youngsters and the kid in all of us. See chapter 7.

THE BEST DRIVE-IN CAMPING

- **Watchman Campground** (Zion National Park): Located just inside the park's south entrance, Watchman Campground has well-spaced sites and lots of trees. In addition, this campground is right on the Pa'rus Trail, providing easy access to practically the entire park. And it even has electric hookups for RVs, a rarity in national parks. See chapter 5.

- **North Campground** (Bryce Canyon National Park): While both of Bryce Canyon National Park's campgrounds offer plenty of trees, providing that genuine "forest camping" experience, North Campground is closer to the Rim Trail than the park's other campground, making it easier to rush over to catch those amazing sunrise colors. See chapter 8.

- **Ruby's Inn RV Park & Campground** (near Bryce Canyon National Park; ✆ **435/834-5301**): For those who want full RV hookups, a woodsy camping experience, lots of amenities, and easy access to the national park, this is the place to be. Part of a giant complex containing a motel, shops, swimming pools, and all sorts of other attractions and activities, this campground has trees and open space as well. See chapter 8.

THE BEST BACKCOUNTRY CAMPING

- **La Verkin Creek/Kolob Arch Trails** (Zion National Park): You'll have to sign up in advance for one of the isolated campsites along this spectacularly scenic trail in the Kolob Canyons. The trail takes you through forests of conifers, cottonwoods, and box elders, past hanging gardens and a series of waterfalls. There is also a side trip to a view of Kolob Arch—at over 300 feet wide, one of the largest natural arches in the world. See chapter 4.

THE BEST LODGING

- **Zion Lodge** (Zion National Park; ✆ **435/772-3213**): The handsome Zion Lodge was built by the Union Pacific Railroad, but tragedy struck in 1966 when it was destroyed by fire. However, it was rebuilt the following year in its original style, and continues to offer the best location for this park's visitors. Situated in a forest with spectacular views of the park's rock cliffs, it offers both cabins and motel rooms. The charming cabins each have a private porch, stone (gas-burning) fireplace, two double beds, and log beams. See chapter 5.

- **Bryce Canyon Lodge** (Bryce Canyon National Park; ℂ 435/834-5361): This handsome sandstone and ponderosa pine lodge is the perfect place to stay while visiting the park. Opened in 1924, it has all the atmosphere of the 1920s, but with most of the modern conveniences people expect today. Especially recommended are its delightful cabins, which have been authentically restored and contain gas-burning stone fireplaces. Those wanting a bit more elegance will enjoy one of the lodge's suites, which are decorated with white wicker furnishings and have ceiling fans and separate sitting areas. See chapter 8.

- **Flanigan's Inn** (near Zion National Park; ℂ 800/765-7787 or 435/772-3244): Made of natural wood and rock, and set among trees, lawns, and flowers just outside the entrance to Zion National Park, this attractive complex has a mountain lodge atmosphere. It's a place where you might actually want to spend some time—unlike some other area options, which are just good places to crash at the end of a busy day. See chapter 5.

- **Snow Family Guest Ranch** (near Zion National Park; ℂ 800/308-7669 or 435/635-2500): A peaceful horse ranch about 12 miles west of Zion National Park's south entrance, this is a welcome alternative to the hustle-and-bustle of motels at the park entrance. Rooms are individually decorated with a western flair and have log furnishings. The large bridal suite has a massive log bed, claw-foot tub, and a separate shower. Guided scenic trail rides are offered for an additional charge. See chapter 5.

- **Best Western Ruby's Inn** (near Bryce Canyon National Park; ℂ 435/834-5341): The motel rooms here are fine—clean and well maintained, with color TVs, telephones, and air-conditioning—but the real reason to stay here is the location, just outside the park entrance. Numerous amenities are offered, from swimming pools and restaurants to shuttle services and plane rides. See chapter 8.

- **Bryce Point Bed & Breakfast** (near Bryce Canyon National Park; ℂ 435/679-8629): The five rooms at this B&B are all unique, each decorated and named for one of Lamar and Ethel LeFevre's children. Consequently, there's a firefighter's room, a commercial airline room, and so forth, all done tastefully and attractively. Most rooms offer beautiful views of Bryce Point through large picture windows, and there is also a handsomely furnished honeymoon cottage. See chapter 8.

THE BEST RESTAURANTS

- **Zion Lodge** (Zion National Park; © **435/772-3213**): You can't beat the view here—large picture windows face the park's magnificent rock formations—and the food is pretty special, too. Try the slow-roasted prime rib au jus or the very popular Utah red mountain trout. See chapter 5.

- **Bryce Canyon Lodge** (Bryce Canyon National Park; © **435/834-5361**): A delightful mountain lodge atmosphere and excellent food make the Bryce Canyon Lodge Dining Room a winner. Decorated with American Indian weavings and baskets, the restaurant has two large stone fireplaces and picture windows looking out at the park. The menu here is similar to that at the Zion Lodge, with house specialties of slow-roasted prime rib au jus and fresh mountain trout, plus chicken dishes and vegetarian items. Then there are the lodge's specialty ice creams and desserts, such as the exotic and very tasty wild "Bryceberry" crumb cake (you won't get that at Zion!). See chapter 8.

- **The Bit & Spur Restaurant & Saloon** (near Zion National Park; © **435/772-3498**): Although this looks like a rough-and-tumble Old West saloon at first glance, it's really a very good restaurant, similar to one of the better restaurants in Santa Fe. The menu includes Mexican standards such as burritos, flautas, and traditional chile stew; but you'll also find more exotic creations. Portions are generous, too. See chapter 5.

THE BEST SIDE TRIPS

- **Cedar Breaks National Monument** (near Cedar City, a side trip from Zion National Park): A delightful little park, Cedar Breaks National Monument is a junior Bryce Canyon, with a spectacular natural amphitheater filled with stone spires, arches, and columns, and painted in reds, purples, oranges, and ochres. Here you can also camp among the spruce, firs, and wildflowers that blanket the 10,000-foot plateau each summer. See chapter 9.

- **Grand Staircase–Escalante National Monument** (near Bryce Canyon National Park): Among America's newest national monuments, this vast wilderness covering some 1.7 million acres is known for its stark, rugged beauty, and particularly its red-orange canyons and deep river valleys. Unlike most other national monuments, almost all of this sweeping area is undeveloped—there are few all-weather roads, only one maintained hiking trail, and two small developed campgrounds. But for the adventurous, there are miles upon miles of dirt roads and practically unlimited opportunities for hiking, horseback riding, camping, and exploring. See chapter 9.

2 A Look at Zion

While it may be easy to conjure up a single defining image of the enormous Grand Canyon or the delicately sculpted rock hoodoos of Bryce, Zion is more difficult to pin down. Here you'll find a collage of images and secrets, an entire smorgasbord of experiences, sights, and even smells, from massive stone sculptures and monuments to lush forests and roaring rivers. Zion is a park to explore, not merely see; take time to walk its trails, visit viewpoints at different times of the day to see the changing light, and let the park work its magic on you.

First established as Mukuntuweap National Monument in 1909—*mukuntuweap* is a Paiute Indian word meaning "straight arrow"—its name was changed to Zion National Monument in 1918, and the area gained national park status the following year. Comprising more than 147,000 acres, the park covers a wide range of elevations—from 3,700 feet to 8,726 feet above sea level—and terrain that runs the gamut from desert to forest, with a dramatic river canyon known as the Narrows thrown in for good measure.

These extremes of elevation have resulted in extremes of climate as well—temperatures in the desert areas soar to well over 100°F in the summer, while higher elevations are sometimes covered with snow and ice in the winter. Due to this variety of conditions, Zion harbors a vast array of plant life, ranging from cactus and yucca to ponderosa pines and cottonwoods. In fact, with almost 800 native species, Zion National Park is said to have the richest diversity of plants in Utah. Be sure to watch for hanging gardens, watered from porous rocks, which you'll see clinging to the sides of cliffs.

Zion is also home to a great variety of animals, drawn here in large part by the year-round water source. Indigenous mammals range from pocket gophers to mountain lions; but you'll also spy hundreds of birds, lizards of all shapes and sizes, and a dozen species of snakes. (Only the Great Basin rattlesnake is poisonous, and it usually slithers away from you faster than you can run from it.)

Mule deer are commonly observed grazing along the forest edges, and practically every park visitor comes across squirrels and chipmunks. A few elk and bighorn sheep may surface, although they're seldom seen. Among the creatures unique to the park is the tiny Zion snail.

Of course, it's not only plants and animals that need water. For some 1,500 years, humans have come here seeking not only water but also the plants and animals that the water nurtures. There is evidence that a group of people known as the Basket Makers lived here as early as A.D. 500, hunting the area's wildlife, gathering berries and seeds, and growing corn, squash, and other crops. They apparently abandoned the area about A.D. 1200, perhaps because of climate changes. Members of the American Indian tribe called the Paiutes—whose descendants still live in southern Utah—are believed to have spent time in what is now the national park, but built no permanent homes. Spanish explorers were in the area in the late 18th century, and American fur traders came in the early 19th century, but there is no evidence that either actually entered Zion Canyon.

Historians believe that it was not until the 1850s that European-Americans finally ventured into Zion Canyon. Probably the first was pioneer Nephi Johnson, who was shown Zion Canyon by Paiutes in November 1858, and for whom Johnson Mountain is named. He was among a group of members of the Church of Jesus Christ of Latter-day Saints (known as Mormons) that was sent from Salt Lake City by church leader Brigham Young in search of arable land. By the early 1860s, the Mormons had begun to establish farms and ranches in the area, near where Zion Lodge is located today and at other locations in what is now the national park. It was early Mormon settler Isaac Behunin who is credited with naming his homestead "Little Zion," because it seemed to him to be a bit of heaven on earth.

In the 1870s, Major John Wesley Powell explored the area, describing in his journals Angels Landing, Court of the Patriarchs, and some of the park's other now-famous landmarks. At about the

---

Impressions

Nothing can exceed the wondrous beauty of Zion . . .
in the nobility and beauty of the sculptures there is no
comparison.

—Geologist Clarence Dutton (1880)

same time, surveyor G. K. Gilbert was mapping southern Utah. He named the Narrows and described it as "the most wonderful defile it has been my fortune to behold."

Today, Zion National Park casts a spell over you as you gaze upon its sheer multicolored walls of sandstone, explore its narrow canyons, search for hanging gardens of ferns and wildflowers, or listen to the roar of the churning, tumbling Virgin River.

3 A Look at Bryce Canyon

One of America's most scenic destinations, Bryce Canyon National Park is a magical land, a place of inspiration and spectacular beauty where thousands of intricately shaped rock formations stir the imagination, as they stand silent watch in their colorful cathedrals. But, perhaps even more important to today's travelers, Bryce Canyon is also one of the West's most accessible national parks. Several trails lead down into the canyon—technically what geologists call an amphitheater—making it relatively easy to get to know this beautiful jewel up close. In addition, there's an easy Rim Trail, part of which is wheelchair accessible, which makes many of the park's best views available to virtually everyone.

The smallest of Utah's five national parks, with an area of just under 36,000 acres, Bryce Canyon was declared a national monument by President Warren Harding in 1923. The following year, Congress passed provisional legislation to create Utah National Park. In 1928 the change in status was finalized and the park was renamed Bryce Canyon National Park, in honor of one of its early residents. It ranges in elevation from 6,620 to 9,115 feet, with desert terrain of piñon, juniper, sagebrush, and cactus at the lower levels, and a cool high country consisting of a dense forest of fir, spruce, and even ancient bristlecone pines. In between, where the campgrounds and visitor center are located, is a ponderosa pine forest.

Bryce Canyon is best known for its hoodoos, which geologists tell us are simply pinnacles of rock, often oddly shaped, left standing after millions of years of water and wind erosion. But perhaps a more interesting explanation lies in a Paiute legend. These American Indians, who lived in the area for several hundred years before being forced out by Anglo pioneers, told of a "Legend People" who lived here in the old days. The powerful Coyote turned them to stone for their evil ways, and even today they remain frozen in time.

Whatever the cause, Bryce Canyon is delightfully unique. Its intricate and often whimsical formations are smaller and on a more

Impressions

*Such glorious tints, such keen contrasts of light and shade . . .
can never be forgotten. . . . This is one of the grand panoramas of the plateau country.*

—Geologist Clarence Dutton (1880)

human scale than the impressive rocks seen at nearby Zion, and Bryce Canyon is far easier to explore than the sometimes intimidating vastness of Grand Canyon National Park. Bryce is comfortable and inviting in its beauty; we feel we know it simply by gazing over the rim, and we're on intimate terms after just one morning on the trail.

Although the colorful hoodoos are the first things that grab your attention, it isn't long before you notice the deep amphitheaters that enfold them, with their cliffs, windows, and arches—all colored in shades of red, brown, orange, yellow, and white—that change and glow with the rising and setting sun. Beyond the rocks and light are the other faces of the park: three separate life zones, each with its own unique vegetation, changing with elevation; and a kingdom of animals, from the busy chipmunks and ground squirrels to stately mule deer and their archenemy, the mountain lion. Also sometimes present in the more remote areas of the park are elk and pronghorn.

It's not known if prehistoric cultures actually saw the wonderful hoodoos at Bryce Canyon, although archaeologists do know Paleo-Indians hunted in the area some 15,000 years ago. By about A.D. 700, the Basket Makers had established small villages in Paria Valley, east of Bryce Canyon in what is now Grand Staircase–Escalante National Monument, also discussed in this book (see chapter 9). By about A.D. 1100, Ancestral Puebloan peoples (also called the Anasazi) were living east of Bryce Canyon, and are believed to have visited what is now the park in search of game and timber.

However, serious exploration of the Bryce area likely began later, with the Paiutes; and it's possible that trappers, prospectors, and early Mormon scouts may have visited here in the early to mid-1800s, before Major John Wesley Powell conducted the first thorough survey of the region in the early 1870s. Shortly after Powell's exploration—in 1875—Mormon pioneer Ebenezer Bryce, a Scottish carpenter, and his wife Mary moved here and tried raising cattle. Their home became known as "Bryce's Canyon." Although they stayed only 5 years before moving to Arizona, Bryce's legacy is his name and his oft-quoted description of the canyon as "a helluva place to lose a cow."

2

Planning Your Trip to Zion & Bryce Canyon National Parks

There once was a time when planning a visit to a national park—particularly those in the western United States—involved little more than choosing the dates and packing the car. You could be assured there would be campsites available, and you usually had the luxury of waiting until you arrived to decide exactly what you wanted to do. Those days are mostly gone; today the wise traveler invests a bit of time before leaving home, not only by reading such books as this one, but also by contacting park offices for maps and information, checking out lodging and camping choices, making reservations, and even researching restaurant, shopping, and side-trip possibilities.

There are several reasons for this. First and foremost is that as more people discover the parks, they are getting more crowded, making it harder to secure campsites, lodging, and even parking. To combat this, it's best to decide what you want to do at the park and then try to schedule your visit for the least-crowded time that is best for those activities. For instance, guided horseback rides are only offered during warmer months, but these are also the busiest times at both parks. Therefore, if horseback riding is something you want to do, schedule your trip for spring or fall, when stables are open, but before or after the busy summer season.

Another good reason for advance planning is that you don't want to waste precious vacation time searching for a motel or campsite vacancy. Luckily, there are far more lodging and dining choices in and near the national parks than there were 10 or 20 years ago. At that time, we were happy if we found a restaurant that was clean and served basic American food. Today, dining out has evolved into an important part of the national park vacation experience.

So don't dread the planning work—like the preparation for any special event, planning a trip to a national park can be a load of fun.

1 Getting Started: Information & Reservations

Start with the national park offices for information on what to see and do, and for current warnings or changes that might not be included in this book, such as road or trail closures.

For advance information on what to see and do in **Zion National Park,** contact the Superintendent, Zion National Park, Springdale, UT 84767-1099 (© **435/772-3256;** www.nps.gov/zion). It's best to write at least a month before your planned visit, and specify what type of information you need. Officials request that those seeking trip-planning information write rather than call.

You can also purchase books, maps, and videos from the non-profit **Zion Natural History Association,** Zion National Park, Springdale, UT 84767 (© **800/635-3959** or 435/772-3264; www.zionpark.org). Some publications are available in foreign languages, and several videos can be purchased in either VHS or PAL formats. Those wanting to help the nonprofit association can join ($35 single or $50 family annually) and get a 20% discount on purchases, plus lesser discounts at many other national park bookstores.

For advance information on what to see and do in **Bryce Canyon National Park,** contact the Superintendent, Bryce Canyon National Park, P.O. Box 170001, Bryce Canyon, UT 84717, or call weekdays between 8am and 4:30pm mountain time (© **435/ 834-5322;** www.nps.gov/brca). It's best to write at least a month before your planned visit, and specify the kind of information you require.

If you desire even more details to help plan your trip, you can order books, maps, posters, and videos (in VHS and PAL formats) from the nonprofit **Bryce Canyon Natural History Association,** Box 170002, Bryce Canyon, UT 84717 (© **888/362-2642** or 435/834-4600; fax 435/834-4102; www.nps.gov/brca/nhamain). The association does not offer memberships, but does give a discount to current members of other national park natural history associations.

LODGING & CAMPING   Both Zion and Bryce Canyon Lodges, which are among the best places to stay while visiting these parks, are often booked months in advance, especially for the busy summer season. Even the basic motels in the parks' gateway towns are often full; therefore we recommend making lodging reservations as early as possible. But even Zion and Bryce Canyon Lodges will sometimes have a last-minute cancellation, so it's worth checking.

Reservations are also recommended for those planning to stay at commercial campgrounds in the gateway towns for both parks, especially if you'll be arriving in the late afternoon or evening. Reservations are not accepted at National Park Service campgrounds at Bryce Canyon, but a reservations system has been implemented at one campground (Watchman) in Zion.

USEFUL PUBLICATIONS Although we have tried to pack as much information as possible into this book, you may want additional information for your trip, especially if you are particularly interested in the area's geology or wildlife, or plan to do a lot of backpacking. The nonprofit natural history associations in both parks (see above) can provide numerous publications that will help you plan your park visit. You'll find detailed trail descriptions covering both parks in *Hiking Zion & Bryce Canyon National Parks* (Helena, Montana: Falcon Press, 1997), by Erik Molvar and Tamara Martin.

Among publications available from the **Zion Natural History Association** are the easy-to-understand 22-page booklet *An Introduction to the Geology of Zion National Park,* by Al Warneke; and *Exploring the Backcountry of Zion National Park: Off-trail Routes,* by Thomas Brereton and James Dunaway. The association also publishes a very useful pocket-size hiking guide, *Zion—The Trails,* compiled by Bob Lineback. Those planning to spend a lot of time on the trails and in the backcountry will want to purchase a copy of the association's topographic map.

The **Bryce Canyon Natural History Association** is a good source for books and maps as well, including the hiking guide mentioned above, *Hiking Zion & Bryce Canyon National Parks.* Published by the association is *The Bryce Canyon Auto and Hiking Guide,* by Tully Stroud and Paul R. Johnson, with discussions of the various viewpoints and hiking trails, and a variety of color photos of the park plus historic black-and-white photos. For those seeking more details on the park's geology, the association publishes *Shadows of Time, The Geology of Bryce Canyon National Park,* 1994, by Frank DeCourten, John Telford, and Hannah Hinchman.

Those planning other stops in Utah during their visit to these national parks should consider purchasing *Frommer's Utah,* also by Don and Barbara Laine, the authors of this book.

2 When to Go

There are a number of factors to consider in choosing when to visit Zion and Bryce Canyon National Parks. Those with children in school will usually have their travel schedules dictated by the school calendar, which means they will be visiting the parks at their busiest times. But this is not necessarily bad, because that's also when both parks offer the largest number of children's activities.

Another consideration is lodging. Rates at and near both parks are higher—sometimes considerably higher—in summer. However, visitors also have more choices in summer since some properties, including the wonderful Bryce Canyon Lodge, close in winter. See chapter 8, "Where to Stay, Camp & Eat in Bryce Canyon," for complete lodging and dining information.

THE CLIMATES

Although Zion and Bryce Canyon National Parks are in the same general area, there are differences in climate as a result of differences in elevation. Zion ranges from 3,700 feet to 8,726 feet, while the elevation at Bryce Canyon starts at 6,620 and rises to 9,115 feet.

Both parks experience all four seasons, although the winters at Zion are relatively mild and little snow falls in the canyon. Weather-wise, spring and fall are the best times to visit Zion, with temperatures ranging from lows in the 40s to pleasant highs in the 80s. Summer daytime highs often soar well above 100°F, with lows dipping only into the 70s. During this time, hiking is best done in the early mornings, especially considering the frequent afternoon thunderstorms in July and August that can change a babbling brook into a raging torrent in minutes.

Because of its higher elevation, Bryce Canyon is almost always cooler than Zion. May through October, daytime temperatures are pleasant—usually from the low 60s to the upper 80s—while nights are cool, dropping into the 40s even at the height of summer. Afternoon thunderstorms are common in July and August. During winter, days are generally clear and crisp, with high temperatures often reaching the 40s, while nights are cold, usually in the single digits or teens, and it is not uncommon to see temperatures well below zero. Snow is common in winter, although park staff plow the roads to the viewpoints.

In both parks, weather conditions may limit some activities at certain times. For instance, at Zion you'll want to avoid long hikes in midsummer, when the park bakes under the desert sun; and at

Bryce Canyon, winter storms can make hiking on steep trails treacherous.

AVOIDING THE CROWDS

Both parks get their highest visitation in summer—particularly during school vacations, from early June to mid-August—and those who prefer fewer people should try to visit at other times.

Zion's quietest months are December, January, and February. Of course, even at relatively warm Zion it's chilly then, and there is the possibility that you may have to contend with some snow and ice (although it rarely lasts). If your schedule permits, many consider it a good compromise to visit in April, May, September, or October, when the weather is usually good but the park is less crowded.

Although Bryce Canyon National Park receives only two-thirds the number of annual visitors that pour into nearby Zion National Park, Bryce can still be crowded, especially during its peak season from mid-June to August. A better time to visit, if your schedule allows, is spring or fall. If you don't mind a bit of cold and snow, the park is practically deserted in the winter—a typical January sees some 22,000 to 25,000 visitors, while in August there are well over 10 times that number—and the sight of bright red hoodoos capped with fresh white snow is something you won't soon forget.

At both parks, there are two other ways to avoid crowds at almost any time of year. First, get started on your explorations as early as possible in the day—preferably just after sunrise. Not only is the light best then and the chance of seeing wildlife much better than later in the day, but you'll practically have the park to yourself, since the majority of visitors don't usually get going until about 10am.

The second way to avoid crowds is simply to walk away from them; most visitors never venture far from the major viewpoints. You can have a wonderful solitary experience if you're willing to expend a little energy. Among the lesser-used day hikes at Bryce Canyon are Fairyland Loop and Peekaboo Loop; and at Zion try the Hop Valley and Observation Point Trails.

At Zion you can also avoid crowds by spending time in Kolob Canyons, in the far northwest section of the park; they're spectacular and receive surprisingly little use, at least in comparison to Zion Canyon. To really get away from humanity at Bryce Canyon, head out on one of the park's two backcountry trails. (See chapter 4 for more day hikes in Zion and chapter 7 for more day hikes at Bryce Canyon.)

✏ A British Invasion

Summer visitors to Zion National Park who want a change of pace can step back to Elizabethan England. It's a much shorter trip than you might think, only 60 miles north to the community of Cedar City for Utah's premier theater event—the **Utah Shakespearean Festival**. The Bard's plays have been professionally staged in this unlikely setting since 1962, and the festival won the prestigious Tony Award for Outstanding Regional Theatre in 2000.

The summer season, which runs from mid-June to August, includes six plays—usually three by Shakespeare and three others—in which top actors perform in true Elizabethan style in an open-air replica of the original Globe Theatre. (If it rains, productions are moved into the adjacent enclosed theater.) Then there are two productions during the fall season, which runs from mid-September to late October.

The plays, however, are only part of the fun. "Royal Feastes," complete with medieval entertainment and winsome serving wenches, are held several evenings each week in summer; the Elizabethan-style prix-fixe dinner is $30 per person. Backstage tours are offered Monday through Saturday for $7. A variety of other programs, including free literary and music seminars and special workshops, are also offered during the summer season.

The festival is held on the Southern Utah University campus, 351 W. Center St., Cedar City, UT 84720. Ticket prices range from $15 to $40, with some matinees starting at $11. For tickets and information, call ✆ **800/PLAYTIX** or 435/586-7878. Tickets can also be ordered (using a credit card) by fax (435/586-1944), e-mail (boxoffice@bard.org), or on the Web (www.bard.org).

SEASONAL EVENTS

Most of the ranger-led activities, such as campfire and amphitheater programs and guided hikes and walks, occur during the summer, although a few are scheduled year-round, such as the once-a-month star-watching program presented at Bryce Canyon. Check the bulletin boards at park visitor centers for current information.

In the Bryce Canyon area, **Ruby's Inn** (© 435/834-5341; www.rubysinn.com) sponsors several events throughout the year (call for the current schedule); and just outside Zion National Park, the **Zion Canyon Chamber of Commerce** (© 888/518-7070; www.zionpark.com) in Springdale can provide information on upcoming events.

IF YOU VISIT IN WINTER

Winter can be especially beautiful in both parks, and is definitely less crowded. Because there are fewer park visitors, rangers will have more time to answer questions and discuss the park's resources. In addition, you're likely to see more of the bigger animals, such as deer and elk, although some of the squirrels and reptiles will be hibernating, and many of the birds will have flown south.

There are disadvantages, of course. For one, far fewer ranger led programs and activities are scheduled in winter. Also, sudden winter

---

✐ What Should I Take?

In packing for your trip, keep in mind that this is a land of extremes, with an often-unforgiving climate and terrain. Those planning to hike or bike should take more drinking water containers than they think they'll need—experts recommend at least 1 gallon of water per person per day on the trail—as well as good quality sunblock, hats and other protective clothing, and sunglasses with ultraviolet protection.

Summer visitors will want to carry rain gear for the typical afternoon thunderstorms, and jackets or sweaters for cool evenings. Winter visitors will not only want warm parkas and hats, but lighter clothing as well—the bright sun at midday can make it feel like June.

Take a first-aid kit, of course, and make sure it contains tweezers—very useful for removing cactus spines from your flesh if you should make the mistake of getting too close. Hikers, especially those planning to go into the Narrows at Zion National Park, will appreciate having a walking stick to brace themselves against the sometimes strong currents on the "trail" that's actually more wading than hiking.

storms can keep you indoors and may leave hiking trails at both parks icy and treacherous. Those going to the parks in winter should carry a variety of clothing that can be worn in layers, to be added or subtracted as conditions change, and make sure to have warm boots with good traction soles. Because the roads getting to and from the parks are mountainous, cars should be equipped with snow tires and should have engine coolant that protects down to 20°F below zero, just in case one of those rare cold fronts moves through.

3 Permits You Can Obtain in Advance

Permits for backcountry trips at both parks can be obtained several days in advance of the planned trip; however, they must be purchased in person at the visitor centers. One exception is at Zion, where permits for overnight trips in the Narrows can be reserved one month in advance (contact park offices for details). Those planning to fish must first purchase state fishing licenses, which are available at sporting goods stores and other businesses throughout Utah. For additional information contact the **Utah Division of Wildlife Resources,** 1594 W. North Temple (P.O. Box 146301), Salt Lake City, UT 84114 (© **877/592-5169** or 801/538-4700; fax 801/538-4745; www.nr.state.ut.us/dwr/dwr.htm), for the current *Utah Fishing Proclamation.* Zion National Park offers limited fishing opportunities; there are no bodies of water appropriate for fishing at Bryce Canyon National Park, although there is fishing nearby (see chapters 4 and 7 on hikes and other outdoor pursuits). Hunting is not permitted in either national park.

4 Getting There

Zion and Bryce Canyon National Parks are 83 miles apart by road.

GETTING TO ZION NATIONAL PARK

Zion National Park is located 46 miles northeast of St. George, 60 miles south of Cedar City, 83 miles southwest of Bryce Canyon National Park, and 120 miles northwest of the north rim of Grand Canyon National Park in northern Arizona. It's 309 miles south of Salt Lake City and 158 miles northeast of Las Vegas, Nevada.

BY CAR   From St. George travel north on I-15 10 miles to exit 16, then east on Utah 9 for 30 miles to the Zion Canyon section of the park. From Salt Lake City take I-15 south to exit 27, then Utah 17 south about 10 miles, and Utah 9 east about 20 miles. Though

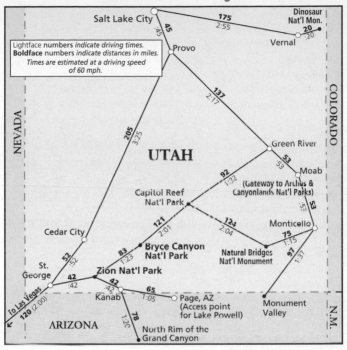

Lightface numbers *indicate driving times.*
Boldface numbers *indicate distances in miles.*
*Times are estimated at a driving speed
of 60 mph.*

less scenic than the eastern approach to the park, this is the easiest route; it's more direct, avoids possible delays at the Zion–Mt. Carmel Tunnel, and delivers you to Springdale, just outside the park's southern entrance, where most of the area's lodging and restaurants are located. (See chapter 5, "Where to Stay, Camp & Eat in Zion.")

The Kolob Canyons section, in the park's northwest corner, is reached via the short Kolob Canyons Road off I-15, exit 40.

From the east it's a spectacularly scenic 24-mile drive from Mt. Carmel Junction on Utah 9 (the Zion–Mt. Carmel Highway), reached from either the north or south via U.S. 89. However, be aware that this route into the park drops over 2,500 feet in elevation, passes through the mile-long Zion–Mt. Carmel Tunnel, and winds down six steep switchbacks. Oversized vehicles are charged $10 for use of the tunnel (see "Regulations" in chapter 3, "Exploring Zion National Park").

Bryce Canyon National Park is north and east of Mt. Carmel Junction via U.S. 89 north (44 miles) and Utah 12 east (13 miles). Kanab is 17 miles southeast of Mt. Carmel Junction along U.S. 89.

BY PLANE   There are small airports at St. George and Cedar City, both located along I-15, and from either it's easy to rent a car and drive to Zion. **Delta/Skywest Airlines** (✆ **800/453-9417**) flies into both airports, and **United Express** (✆ **800/241-6522**) serves St. George.

Car-rental agencies with St. George offices include **ABC** (✆ 435/628-7355); **Allsave** (✆ 435/628-1800), **Avis** (✆ 435/634-3940); **Budget** (✆ 435/673-6825); **Enterprise** (✆ 435/634-1556); and **Hertz** (✆ 435/652-9941). Car-rental agencies at the Cedar City Airport include **National** (✆ 435/586-7059) and **Avis** (✆ 435/586-3033). Transportation from St. George and Cedar City to the park is available from **Zion Canyon Transportation** (✆ 877/635-5993 or 435/635-5993), which also provides local taxi service in the Springdale area.

The closest major airport is **McCarran International Airport** in Las Vegas, Nevada (✆ **702/261-5211;** www.mccarran.com), which is about 120 miles southwest of St. George via I-15. Most major airlines fly into McCarran, and most major car-rental agencies have outlets at the airport. The **St. George Shuttle** (✆ **800/933-8320** or 435/628-8320; www.stgshuttle.com) provides daily service between St. George and the Las Vegas airport.

GETTING TO BRYCE CANYON NATIONAL PARK

Bryce Canyon National Park is 50 miles west of Escalante, 80 miles east of Cedar City, 83 miles northeast of Zion National Park, 120 miles southwest of Capitol Reef National Park, 135 miles northeast of St. George, and 160 miles north of the north rim of Grand Canyon National Park in northern Arizona. It's about 250 miles south of Salt Lake City.

BY CAR   From Zion National Park, head east on Utah 9 about 18 miles to U.S. 89, north 44 miles to Utah 12, and east 17 miles to the park entrance road (Utah 63). The Entrance Station is just 3 miles south of Utah 12.

From St. George travel north on I-15 10 miles to exit 16, east on Utah 9 for 63 miles to U.S. 89, north 44 miles to Utah 12, and east 17 miles to the park entrance road.

From Capitol Reef National Park, take Utah 24 west 10 miles to Torrey, turn southwest onto Scenic Highway Utah 12, through Boulder and Escalante, for about 110 miles to the park entrance road.

From Salt Lake City take I-15 south about 200 miles to exit 95, east 13 miles on Utah 20, south on U.S. 89 for 17 miles to Utah 12, and east 17 miles to the park entrance road.

BY PLANE   The closest airport with regularly scheduled flights is at Cedar City (see above).

Bryce Canyon Airport (© 435/834-5239), at 7,586 feet elevation, is located several miles from the park entrance on Utah 12, and has a 7,400-foot lighted runway. Charter service is available from **Bryce Canyon Airlines** (© 435/834-5050). Car rentals are available from **Bryce Canyon Car Rental** (© 800/432-5383 or 435/834-5200).

5 Tips for RVers

One of the best ways to explore Zion and Bryce Canyon National Parks, especially in warmer months, is in an RV or in a car or truck while spending your nights in a tent—assuming you don't mind roughing it a bit.

One advantage to this type of travel is that early morning and early evening are among the best times to be in these parks, and it's a lot more convenient to experience the parks at these times if you're already there, staying in one of the park campgrounds. Another reason to camp is that if you have special dietary requirements, you won't have to worry about trying to find a restaurant that can meet your needs; you'll be able to cook for yourself, either in your RV or on a camp stove.

But the best reason is simply that inexplicable feeling of contentment that comes from waking up to the sound of birds singing and furry little creatures scurrying about outside your door; you're living the national park experience rather than just visiting as if it were an amusement park.

There are disadvantages, of course. Tents, small trailers, and even the most luxurious motor homes and fifth-wheel trailers provide somewhat close quarters. Facilities in national park campgrounds are limited, although they are being upgraded. Even in most commercial campgrounds, the facilities are less than you'd expect in moderately priced motels. But, all this aside, camping is just plain fun—especially in settings as spectacular as Zion and Bryce Canyon.

There are a few things that RVers might want to know. Entering Zion from the east in an RV will involve an extra fee and probably a wait to get through the Zion–Mt. Carmel Tunnel, and there may be parking restrictions. However, you'll find that taking your RV into these parks isn't that much of a hassle, especially if you plan ahead.

For instance, parking is limited, especially for motor homes and other large vehicles, so take shuttle busses as much as possible, and drive either early or late in the day, when there's less traffic.

If you'll be traveling in the parks in your RV and want to make it obvious that your campsite is occupied, carry something to leave in it, such as a cardboard box with "Site Taken" clearly written on it.

Because many of the national park campsites are not level, carry four or five short boards, or leveling blocks, that can be placed under the RV's wheels. You can buy small, inexpensive levels at RV and hardware stores, and you'll discover that not only will you sleep better if your rig is level, but your food won't slide off the table and the refrigerator will run more efficiently.

Once you've got an RV or tent, you'll need a place to put it, of course. Elsewhere in this book you'll find information on camping in Zion and Bryce Canyon National Parks, on nearby federal and state lands, and in the parks' gateway towns. Those planning to camp elsewhere in the state can get information on Utah's national forests from the **U.S. Forest Service Regional Office,** Federal Building 324, 25th St., Ogden, UT 84401 (© **801/625-5306;** fax 801/625-5127; www.fs.fed.us/r4). The Utah State Office of the **U.S. Bureau of Land Management** is at 324 S. State St., Suite 301 (P.O. Box 45155), Salt Lake City, UT 84145-0155 (© **801/539-4001;** www.blm.gov/utah). For information on Utah's state parks, contact **Utah State Parks and Recreation,** 1594 W. North Temple, Suite 116 (P.O. Box 146001), Salt Lake City, UT 84114-6001 (© **800/322-3770,** or 801/538-7220 for campground reservations; http://parks.state.ut.us).

Members of the **American Automobile Association (AAA)** can request the club's free *Southwestern CampBook,* which includes campgrounds and RV parks in Utah, Arizona, Colorado, and New Mexico. And several massive campground directories can be purchased in major bookstores, including *Trailer Life Campgrounds, RV Parks, & Services* (www.tldirectory.com) and *Woodall's Campground Directory* (www.woodalls.com).

6 Adventure Vacations & Organized Tours

A number of nationally recognized organizations offer tours and other activities that include the Zion and Bryce Canyon National Park areas, although not necessarily within the park boundaries. In

Renting an RV for Your National Park Trek

If you own an RV, you're all set for a trip to Zion and Bryce Canyon National Parks; but if you don't, you might want to consider renting one.

But first, let's get one thing straight: You probably won't save a lot of money. It is possible to travel fairly cheaply if you limit your equipment to a tent, a pop-up tent trailer, or a small pickup truck camper, but renting a motor home will probably end up costing almost as much as driving a compact car, staying in moderately priced motels, and eating in family-style restaurants and cafes. That's because the motor home will go only one third as far on a gallon of gas as your compact car, and they're expensive to rent (generally between $1,000 and $1,100 per week in mid-summer, when rates are highest).

But carrying your house with you gives you the opportunity to stay in the national park campgrounds, which many park visitors believe is one of the highlights of their trip. It also lets you stop for meals anytime and anywhere you choose. An added benefit is that you won't spend time searching for a restroom—almost all RVs have some sort of bathroom facilities.

If you're planning to fly into the area and rent an RV when you arrive, choose your starting point carefully. Not only will you want to keep the driving to a minimum, but also rental rates vary, depending on the city in which you pick up your RV. Rental rates are usually less in Las Vegas, Nevada, than in Salt Lake City, and most of Utah's national parks are closer to Las Vegas than Salt Lake City anyway.

The country's largest RV rental company, with outlets in Las Vegas and Salt Lake City, is **Cruise America** (© 800/327-7799; fax 602/464-7321; www.cruiseamerica.com). RV rentals are also available from **El Monte RV** (© 888/337-2214 or 562/483-4956; www.elmonte.com). Information on additional rental agencies, as well as tips on renting, can be obtained from the **Recreation Vehicle Rental Association,** 3930 University Dr., Fairfax, VA 22030 (© **703/591-7130;** www.rvra.org).

most cases, all you do is pay and they arrange everything, including lodging, meals, and transportation. These range from fairly standard bus tours to adventure vacations where you spend your days hiking or biking, but are pampered with gourmet meals, hot tubs, and first-class hotels at night. You'll want to contact these operators as far in advance as possible, since reservations are required, and group sizes are limited. The adventure tour operators generally specialize in small groups and have trips for various levels of ability and physical condition. Trips are offered in a range of price categories, from basic to luxurious, and are of varying lengths.

For a complete list of outfitters in Utah, as well as a lot of other useful information and Web links, contact the **Utah Travel Council,** Council Hall, Salt Lake City, UT 84114 (✆ **800/ 200-1160** or 801/538-1030; fax 801/538-1399; www.utah.com). Well-respected national companies that offer tours to southern Utah's national parks include **Maupintour** (✆ **800/255-4266;** www.maupintour.com) and **Tauck Tours** (✆ **800/788-7885;** www.tauck.com).

- **American Orient Express Railway Company,** 2025 First Ave., Suite 830, Seattle, WA 98121 (✆ **888/759-3944** or 206/441-2725; www.americanorientexpress.com), offers a luxurious excursion from Santa Fe to Salt Lake City that includes side trips to Zion and Bryce Canyon National Parks. You'll travel in trains with restored vintage passenger cars outfitted in polished mahogany and brass, dining cars decked out with china, silver, crystal, and linen, and a cuisine to match.
- **Austin-Lehman Adventures,** P.O. Box 81025, Billings, MT 59108-1025 (✆ **800/575-1540** or 406/655-4591; fax 406/651-9236; www.austinlehman.com), a merger of Backcountry and Adventures Plus, offers guided multi-day mountain biking, hiking, and combination tours in the Zion and Bryce Canyon National Parks area.
- **Backroads,** 801 Cedar St., Berkeley, CA 94710-1800 (✆ **800/ 462-2848** or 510/527-1555; fax 510/527-1444; www.back roads.com), offers a variety of guided multi-day road biking, mountain biking, and hiking tours to the national parks in southern Utah.
- **Bicycling Adventures,** P.O. Box 11219, Olympia, WA 98508 (✆ **800/443-6060** or 360/786-0989; fax 360/786-9661; www.bicycleadventures.com), offers guided multi-day hiking

and biking excursions in the Zion and Bryce Canyon National Parks area.

- **GORPtravel,** P.O. Box 1486, Boulder, CO 80306 (© 877/ 532-4677; fax 303/635-0658; www.gorptravel.com), formerly American Wilderness Experience, offers mountain biking, hiking, four-wheeling, horseback riding, and rafting excursions plus cattle drives throughout the West, including multi-day trips in the Bryce Canyon area.

- **Gray Line Motor Tours,** 553 W. 100 South, Salt Lake City, UT 84101 (© **800/309-2352** or 801/521-7060; www. grayline.com), offers several tours of Salt Lake City and the surrounding area, plus national-park packages in the summer, including a 3-day, 2-night trip to Zion and Bryce Canyon National Parks and Grand Canyon National Park.

- **The World Outdoors,** 2840 Wilderness Place, Suite F, Boulder, CO 80301 (© **800/488-8483** or 303/413-0938; fax 303/413-0926; www.theworldoutdoors.org), formerly Roads Less Traveled, offers a variety of trips including multi-sport adventures that include hiking, mountain biking, horseback riding, and rafting to the Canyonlands area, plus hiking/biking trips to Bryce Canyon, Zion, and the north rim of Grand Canyon National Parks.

7 Tips for Travelers with Disabilities

Both Zion and Bryce Canyon National Parks have made great strides in the past few years in making their facilities more accessible to those with disabilities. Visitor centers at both parks are wheelchair accessible, including the restrooms. At Bryce Canyon, a half-mile section of the Rim Trail, between Sunrise and Sunset Points, is fairly level, paved, and wheelchair accessible; several of the viewpoints along the scenic drive are accessible; the Bristlecone Loop Trail at Rainbow Point has a hard surface and is accessible with assistance; and Sunset Campground has accessible campsites. In Zion, accessible campsites are available in South Campground; Riverside Walk at the end of Zion Canyon Scenic Drive is paved and accessible with assistance; Pa'rus Trail is a 2-mile paved and accessible trail, open also to bicyclists. In addition, rangers at both parks are extremely receptive to helping visitors with disabilities.

The National Park Service's **Golden Access Passport,** available free at all national parks, is a lifetime pass that is issued to any U.S.

citizen or permanent resident who is medically certified as disabled or blind. The pass permits free entry and gives a 50% discount on park service campgrounds and activities, but it does not cover user fees or charges for services offered by private concessionaires.

The Utah information and referral line for people with disabilities is ℂ **800/333-8824.**

Amtrak will, with 24 hours' notice, provide porter service, special seating, and a discount (ℂ **800/USA-RAIL**). If you're traveling with a companion, **Greyhound** will carry you both for a single fare (ℂ **800/231-2222**). Both Amtrak and Greyhound have scheduled stops in St. George and Cedar City.

Many of the major car-rental companies now offer hand-controlled cars for disabled drivers, and can provide those vehicles with advance notice. **Wheelchair Getaways** (ℂ **800/642-2042** or 859/873-4973; www.wheelchair-getaways.com) rents specialized vans with wheelchair lifts and other features for drivers with disabilities, with outlets in most of the southwestern states.

8 Tips for Travelers with Pets

National parks, including Zion and Bryce Canyon, are not pet-friendly, and those planning to visit the parks should consider leaving their pets at home. Pets are prohibited on hiking trails, in the backcountry, and in all buildings, and must always be on a leash no more than 6 feet long. One happy exception is at Zion, where leashed pets are permitted on the Pa'rus Trail. Pets should not be left unattended in campgrounds at either park. Essentially, this means that if you take your pet into the parks they can be with you in the campgrounds and inside your vehicle, and you can walk them in parking areas, but that's about it.

Special Tip for Pet Owners

Although pets are not permitted on practically any of the trails or in the backcountry in Bryce Canyon and Zion National Parks, those traveling with their dogs can hike with them over miles of trails administered by the U.S. Forest Service and Bureau of Land Management, adjacent to both national parks. Pets are also welcome, even on trails, in Grand Staircase–Escalante National Monument (administered by the BLM) and in Utah's state parks (see chapter 9, "Nearby Things to See & Do").

Aside from regulations, though, you need to be concerned with your pet's well-being. Pets should never be left in closed vehicles, where temperatures can soar to over 120°F in minutes, resulting in brain damage or death, and there is no punishment too severe for the human who subjects a dog or cat to that torture. At this writing, there are no boarding kennels within 80 miles of Bryce Canyon National Park. Pet boarding is available in several communities near Zion; contact the **park office** (✆ **435/772-3256**) for current information.

Those who do decide to take pets with them into these parks despite the above warnings should take the pets' leashes (of course); carry plenty of water (pet shops sell clever little travel water bowls that won't spill in a moving vehicle); and proof that the dogs or cats have been vaccinated against rabies. Flea and tick spray or powder is also important, especially if you will be taking your pet to Bryce Canyon, where bubonic plague is transmitted by the fleas of prairie dogs and other rodents (see chapter 6, "Exploring Bryce Canyon National Park").

9 Tips for Travelers with Children

Visiting Zion and Bryce Canyon National Parks with your children can be an especially rewarding experience, and is an excellent way for everyone to learn about the parks' geology, plants, and animals, as well as to appreciate the unequaled beauty of nature.

However, these parks are in remote areas, and their gateway cities are little more than small towns. There are no major chain grocery or discount stores, and although you will be able to buy items such as baby food and disposable diapers, you may not find the variety that you're used to. Parents should carry a good supply of these items with them, or stock up before they leave larger communities such as Salt Lake City or St. George. It's also a good idea to carry any prescription drugs you might need, and also to make sure you have the phone numbers of your doctor and pharmacist.

10 Protecting Your Health & Safety

The rugged landscapes that make Zion and Bryce Canyon such beautiful destinations can also be hazardous. Since the isolation of many of the areas you'll seek out means there may be no one there to help in an emergency, the answer is to be prepared, like any good Boy Scout (see box entitled "What Should I Take?," earlier in this chapter). Most importantly, before heading out check with park offices and park rangers about current conditions.

Southern Utah's extremes of **climate**—from burning desert to snow-covered mountains—can produce health problems if you're not prepared. If you haven't been to the desert before, it can be difficult to comprehend the heat, dryness, and intensity of the sun. If you're prone to dry skin, moisturizing lotion is a must; even if you're not, you will probably end up using it. Everyone needs to use a good quality sunblock, wear a hat, and wear sunglasses with full ultraviolet protection. Hikers and others planning to be outside will also need to carry water—at least a gallon per person per day is recommended.

The other potential problem is **elevation.** Bryce Canyon National Park rises to over 9,000 feet, and a side trip to Cedar Breaks National Monument (see chapter 9, "Nearby Things to See & Do") will take you to over 10,000 feet. These elevations are high enough to produce health problems for those not accustomed to them—there's less oxygen and lower humidity up there than many visitors are used to. In fact, the most common complaint at the first-aid station at Bryce Canyon Lodge is shortness of breath. Those with heart or respiratory problems should consult their doctors before planning a trip to these parks, Bryce Canyon in particular. If you're in generally good health, you don't need to take any special precautions, but it's advisable to ease into high elevations by changing altitude gradually. Also, get plenty of rest, avoid large meals, and drink plenty of nonalcoholic fluids, especially water.

State health officials also warn outdoor enthusiasts to take precautions against the **Hantavirus,** a rare but often fatal respiratory disease, first recognized in 1993. About half of the country's confirmed cases have been reported in the Four Corners states of Colorado, New Mexico, Arizona, and Utah. The droppings and urine of rodents usually spread the disease, and health officials recommend that campers and hikers avoid areas with signs of rodent occupation. Symptoms of Hantavirus are similar to flu, and lead to breathing difficulties and shock.

Other park-specific problems are bubonic plague, which is discussed in chapter 6, "Exploring Bryce Canyon National Park," and flash flooding, which is discussed in chapter 4, "Hikes & Other Outdoor Pursuits in Zion National Park."

11 Protecting the Environment

Many of the wonderful outdoor areas you'll be exploring in Zion and Bryce Canyon National Parks are quite isolated, especially in the backcountry at Zion. Not long ago, the rule of thumb was to "leave only footprints"; these days, we're trying to do better and not leave even footprints. It's relatively easy to be a good outdoor citizen—pack out all trash, stay on established trails, be especially careful not to pollute water, and, in general, do your best to have as little impact on the environment as possible. Some hikers carry a small trash bag to pick up what others may have left. As the park service says, protecting our national parks is everyone's responsibility.

3

Exploring Zion National Park

Utah's most popular national park, Zion is a spectacularly beautiful spot, where you'll discover a wide variety of sights and experiences. Here you'll see the minute Zion snail—almost too small to see at all—and a variety of birds and other creatures of practically all shapes and sizes. Massive rock formations, such as the Great White Throne, give one the feeling that this is something permanent, but the beautiful Narrows, where time and water have carved huge chunks of stone into a delicate work of art, prove otherwise.

1 Essentials

ACCESS/ENTRY POINTS   Zion National Park has two main sections: **Zion Canyon,** the main part of the park, and the less-visited **Kolob Canyons.** The main east-west road through Zion Canyon is the park-owned extension of Utah 9; from here the park's 14-mile round-trip Zion Canyon Scenic Drive heads north, providing access to most scenic overlooks and trail heads.

Utah 9 crosses Zion National Park, giving the main section of the park two entry gates—south and east. The south entrance, at Springdale, is by far the more popular, with two-thirds of park visitors arriving there. Most area lodging and restaurants are found in Springdale (see chapter 5, "Where to Stay, Camp & Eat in Zion"). In addition, the park's two campgrounds and the Zion Canyon Visitor Center are located just inside the south entrance.

There is no town at the east entrance, but that route is more scenic—it drops over 2,500 feet in elevation, passes through the mile-long Zion–Mt. Carmel Tunnel, and winds down six steep switchbacks. The tunnel is too small for two-way traffic that includes vehicles larger than standard passenger cars and pickup trucks, so oncoming traffic must be stopped to let them through (see "Regulations," below). Those also visiting Bryce Canyon National Park will probably enter or leave Zion through the east entrance.

Tips **Where to Find Restrooms in Zion**

The all-important restrooms at Zion are generally well maintained, but vary considerably in the facilities offered. As at most national parks, the best are at the visitor centers, where you'll find heated rooms with flush toilets and sinks. There are also public restrooms at the Zion Lodge shuttle stop. South and Watchman Campgrounds, the Grotto Picnic Area, and the Temple of Sinawava Trail Head have flush toilets and sinks. Lava Point Campground, Kolob Canyons Viewpoint, and Weeping Rock and Canyon Overlook Trail Heads have vault toilets. Although essentially outhouses, this type of facility has come a long way in the past 20 years—they're clean, sanitary, and best of all they don't smell. However, there are no lights, no water for hand washing, and no heat. There are no toilets along trails or in the backcountry.

During busy times, some facilities may run out of toilet paper, so it's best to carry a backup supply.

The **Kolob Canyons** section, in the park's northwest corner, is easily reached on the short Kolob Canyons Road off I-15, at exit 40.

About 15 miles west of Zion Canyon, Kolob Terrace Road heads north from the village of Virgin off Utah 9, providing access to several backcountry trails (see chapter 4, "Hikes & Other Outdoor Pursuits in Zion National Park") and the Lava Point Campground (see chapter 5, "Where to Stay, Camp & Eat in Zion"). This road is closed in the winter.

To get to Bryce Canyon National Park, head north and east on Utah 9, U.S. 89, and Utah 12.

VISITOR CENTERS & INFORMATION   The park has two visitor centers. The new **Zion Canyon Visitor Center & Transportation Hub** (© 435/772-3256), near the south entrance to the park, has a wide variety of outdoor exhibits. Rangers answer questions and provide backcountry permits, free brochures are available, and books, maps, videos, postcards, and posters are sold. The **Kolob Canyons Visitor Center** (© 435/586-9548), in the northwest corner of the park off I-15, provides information, permits, books, and maps. Both visitor centers are open from 8am to 7pm in summer, with shorter hours the rest of the year.

Zion National Park

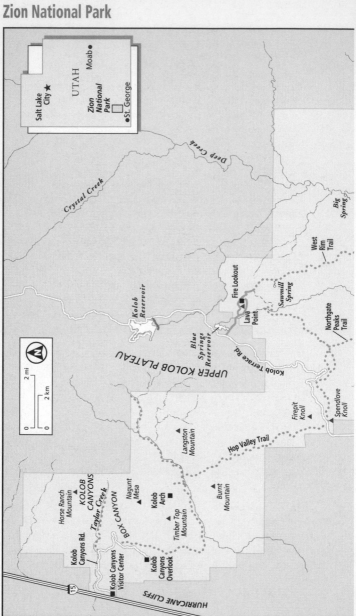

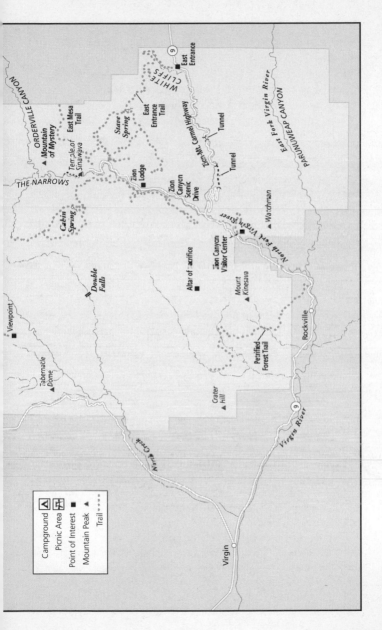

Campground ▲
Picnic Area ⊞
Point of Interest ■
Mountain Peak ▲
Trail •••••

ORDERVILLE CANYON

THE NARROWS

Mountain
of Mystery ▲

Temple of
Sinawava

East Mesa
Trail

Statue
Spring

East
Entrance
Trail

WHITE
CLIFFS

East Entrance

9

Cabin
Spring

Zion
Lodge

Zion Canyon
Scenic
Drive

Zion-Mt. Camel Highway

Tunnel

Tunnel

East Fork Virgin River

PARUNUWEAP CANYON

North Fork Virgin River

Watchman ▲

Double
Falls

Altar of Sacrifice
■

Zion Canyon
Visitor Center ■

Mount
Kinesava ▲

Viewpoint ■

Tabernacle
Dome ▲

Petrified
Forest Trail

North Creek

Rockville ○

Crater
Hill ▲

9

Virgin ○

Virgin River

In addition, plans are underway to open a new **Human History Museum** at the site of the old Zion Canyon Visitor Center in summer 2002.

FEES Entry into the park (for up to 7 days), which includes unlimited use of the shuttle bus, costs $20 per private vehicle or $10 per individual on motorcycle, bicycle, or on foot (maximum charge of $20 per family). National Park, Golden Eagle, Golden Access, and Golden Age passes are honored. Oversized vehicles are charged $10 for use of the Zion–Mt. Carmel Tunnel on the east side of the park (see "Regulations," below).

Permits, available at either visitor center, are required for all overnight trips into the backcountry. Cost is $5 per person per night. Camping costs $14 per night for basic campsites and $16 per night for sites with electric hookups (located in Watchman Campground).

REGULATIONS The mile-long Zion–Mt. Carmel Tunnel (see "Historic & Man-Made Attractions," later in this chapter) is too small for two-way traffic that includes vehicles larger than standard passenger cars and pickup trucks. Buses, trucks, and most recreational vehicles must be driven down the center of the tunnel, and therefore all oncoming traffic must be stopped. This applies to all vehicles over 7'10" wide (including mirrors) or 11'4" tall (including luggage racks and so forth). For affected vehicles, there is a $10 fee, good for two trips through the tunnel during a 7-day period, which is paid at the entrance stations. Hours for escorts are limited during winter months (get details at park entrances or by calling park headquarters). All vehicles over 13'1" tall and certain other particularly large vehicles are prohibited from driving anywhere on the park road between the east entrance and Zion Canyon.

Bicycles are prohibited in the Zion–Mt. Carmel Tunnel, the backcountry, and on trails, except the Pa'rus Trail. Feeding or molesting wildlife, vandalism, and disturbing any natural feature of the park is forbidden. Dogs, which must be leashed at all times, are prohibited on all trails (except the Pa'rus Trail, where leashed pets are permitted), in the backcountry, and in public buildings.

Backcountry hikers should practice minimum impact techniques and are prohibited from building fires. A limit on the number of people allowed in various parts of the backcountry may be in force during your visit; prospective backcountry hikers should check with rangers before setting out. A free booklet on backcountry travel, available at the visitor centers, lists all regulations plus descriptions of close to 20 backcountry trails.

✒ *FAST FACTS:* Zion National Park

ATMs The closest automated teller machine (ATM) to the park is at the **Zion Canyon Theatre Complex** (✆ 435/772-2400), just outside the south entrance, at 145 Zion Park Blvd. There is also an ATM at **Zions Bank**, 921 Zion Park Blvd. (✆ 435/772-3274).

Car Trouble/Towing Services Emergency 24-hour service is available from **W. J. Bassett Repair** (✆ 435/772-3328) in Springdale.

Emergencies Dial ✆ **911** or **435/772-3322** 24 hours a day, or locate the nearest park ranger.

Gas Stations **Springdale Chevron** is located on the south side of town at 1593 Zion Park Blvd. ((✆ **435/772-3922**). Just outside the east entrance to the park, there is a gas station at the **Zion Mt. Carmel Restaurant** (✆ 435/648-2829).

Laundry There are no laundry facilities in Zion National Park, but coin-operated laundries are located at **Zion Canyon Campground** (✆ 435/772-3237), just outside the park's east entrance, and in downtown Springdale in the **Zion Park Motel** complex (✆ 435/772-3251). Just outside the park's east entrance, there is a coin-operated laundry at **Mukuntuweep RV Park & Campground** (✆ 435/648-2154).

Medical Services The **Zion Medical Clinic**, 120 Lion Blvd., Springdale (✆ 435/772-3226) is open daily May through October, and about 1 day a week the rest of the year. For medical emergencies, dial ✆ **911** or **435/772-3322**, or locate the nearest park ranger. One of the larger hospitals in this part of the state is **Dixie Regional Medical Center**, 544 S. 400 E., St. George ((✆ 435/634-4000). From the east entrance, the nearest medical facility is the **Kane County Hospital and Skilled Nursing Facility**, 335 N. Main St., Kanab (✆ 435/644-5811).

Permits Permits, available at the visitor centers, are required for overnight backcountry camping (see "Fees," under "Essentials," above), and special permits are also necessary to drive RVs and other large vehicles through the Zion–Mt. Carmel Tunnel (see "Regulations," under "Essentials," above).

Post Offices There is a post office inside Zion Lodge (ZIP 84767) and mail drops at each of the visitor centers. Springdale's post office (ZIP 84767) is located at 624 Zion Park Blvd. (✆ 800/275-8777 for hours and other post office locations).

Supplies You'll find most of the groceries and camping and RV supplies you want in Springdale, just outside the park's south entrance. At **Zion Canyon Campground,** on Zion Park Boulevard a half mile south of the park's south entrance (✆ 435/772-3237) is a store with groceries, souvenirs, and RV supplies, plus a restaurant. In downtown Springdale, the **Zion Park Market,** 855 Zion Park Blvd. (✆ 435/772-3251), stocks a good selection of groceries, plus has video rentals. On the south end of Springdale on Utah 9 (the opposite side of town from the national park), is the highly recommended **Springdale Fruit Company** (✆ 435/772-3222), which sells fresh organic fruits, vegetables, and juices (try the fruit smoothies), plus trail mix and baked goods. It also has a picnic area. The **Switchback C-Store,** 1149 S. Zion Park Blvd. (✆ 435/772-3700), stocks snacks and pastries and contains the local **state liquor store.** Those in need of outdoor equipment, hiking boots, clothing, and the like will find what they need at **Zion Outdoor,** 868 Zion Park Blvd. (✆ 435/772-0630).

Just outside the east entrance to the park, there is a small store and gas station at **Zion Mt. Carmel Restaurant** (✆ 435/648-2829).

Telephones Public telephones are located at the visitor center, Zion Lodge, and both Watchman and South campgrounds.

Weather For current statewide weather information, contact the **National Weather Service** (✆ 801/524-5133; http://nimbo.wrh.noaa.gov/saltlake). For local weather information, call the park office at ✆ 435/772-3256, Monday through Friday from 8am to 4:30pm.

2 Tips from a Park Ranger

"Overpowering, but also intimate" is how former backcountry Ranger Dave Rachlis sees Zion National Park, adding, "These are some of the highest vertical rock walls that some people will ever see."

An added bonus is an extensive and highly accessible trail system, much of which was constructed in the 1920s and 1930s. "The park has a sense of grandeur, but then it also has access," says Rachlis. "You can go up the West Rim Trail or you can go up the East Rim

Trail, and you can get into these narrow canyons, and really experience the park pretty easily."

Rachlis says that most visitors to Zion see only a small part of the park—what's visible from the viewpoints—but he recommends that visitors stay at least a full day, adding, "In 2 or 3 days, you can see most of the major regions of the park, and get a chance to get out on the trails a bit for day hikes." Those who want to explore the backcountry will need more time.

A hike through the Narrows is "the ultimate slot canyon experience," says Rachlis. "You're following a drainage, wading or swimming in a river in spots—in summer it's one of the cooler areas of the park." He adds, "One of the unique aspects of the Narrows is that the river runs year-round."

Rachlis also recommends the relatively easy La Verkin Creek Trail, which leads to Kolob Arch, believed to be the world's largest freestanding arch. "It's very intimate, very colorful—the rock is a little more orange-to-red than it is in the main canyon." For the best scenery, Rachlis directs people to the West Rim Trail, which gets you up onto the plateau where you can look down into the canyons.

One mistake some park visitors make, Rachlis says, is to downplay the dangers of the easy and moderate hiking trails, where most injuries occur. He says that people understand the hazards on difficult trails such as Angels Landing, where you're inching along a knife-edge ridge; but you also need to be careful on trails with less-obvious dangers. "Sandstone is slippery, and a 20-foot fall can kill you as easily as a 1,000-foot fall."

Zion National Park has a growing reputation as a destination for rock climbers, but Rachlis says this is not the place for beginners. "There are no bolts placed on the walls for the most part; it's free climbing, where people put their own anchoring in and then pull it out as they go up. Because of the softness of the rock, the difficulty of the crack systems here, it's not recommended for casual climbers—it's an expert climber's paradise." He recommends that those with less than expert rock climbing skills go to Snow Canyon State Park (see chapter 9, "Nearby Things to See & Do").

As for when to visit, Rachlis says the trails can be hot in summer, so the best time for hiking is probably spring and fall—from April to June and from September to November. The park is also less crowded then. But he adds that the park has unpredictable weather, so it's best to call to check on current conditions before showing up ready to hike.

3 The Highlights

There is such a wide variety of things to do and see here that it's difficult to say which are the highlights, but probably the single most important activity for visitors is traveling the **Zion Canyon Scenic Drive** 🐾🐾 (by shuttle bus in summer, your car in winter) stopping at viewpoints where you can see many of the park's best-known rock formations.

Among the spectacular rock formations you won't want to miss is **the Great White Throne** 🐾🐾🐾, which can be seen from Zion Canyon Scenic Drive as well as from several hiking trails, including Observation Point Trail, Deertrap Mountain Trail, Angels Landing Trail, and Emerald Pools Trail (see chapter 4, "Hikes & Other Outdoor Pursuits in Zion National Park"). Considered the symbol of Zion National Park for many visitors, this massive and imposing block of Navajo sandstone towers 2,000 feet above the North Fork of the Virgin River. It can be especially impressive when colored by the setting sun. A postage stamp depicting the Great White Throne was issued in the 1930s.

Another eye-catcher is the huge **Checkerboard Mesa,** which you pass when entering the park from the east. Looking as though some giant hand etched it, this huge dome of sandstone has a fishnet pattern created by a unique form of erosion and weathering. Although horizontal lines in Navajo sandstone are fairly common, the rare vertical lines are believed to have been formed by freezing and thawing processes, and then enlarged by running water. For more information see "Seeing the Park by Car and Shuttle," later in this chapter.

Those who think of southern Utah as nothing but burning desert will learn differently at **Weeping Rock,** a short but steep walk along Weeping Rock Trail. Its name derives from the fact that water continually runs down the vertical face of the rock, nurturing hanging gardens. For more, see chapter 4, "Hikes & Other Outdoor Pursuits in Zion National Park," and chapter 10, "A Nature Guide to Zion & Bryce Canyon National Parks."

The **Emerald Pools** 🐾🐾 provide another look at the wet side of Zion—lush green plants, pretty pools of water, and two delightful cascading waterfalls. Located in a short canyon near Zion Lodge, the lower pool is an easy walk along a paved path, while the two upper pools require a bit of real hiking. The pools are named for their rich green color, the result of algae in the water. You'll find more information in chapter 4, "Hikes & Other Outdoor Pursuits in Zion National Park."

At the end of the Zion Canyon Scenic Drive is the **Temple of Sinawava,** a picturesque canyon surrounded by rock walls reaching 2,000 feet into the sky. Here, you'll discover the aptly named Pulpit and Altar rock formations, as well as maple and cottonwood trees and a spectacular seasonal waterfall that cascades almost 1,000 feet down the temple's west wall. This is the beginning of the Riverside Walk, discussed below and in chapter 4, "Hikes & Other Outdoor Pursuits in Zion National Park."

The **Riverside Walk** ★★★, one of the park's easiest trails, should not be ignored just because it's not a challenge. It begins at the Temple of Sinawava and parallels the Virgin River, providing a good sense of the steepness of the canyon walls as you approach the Narrows. Along the walk are interpretative signs discussing this particular ecosystem. This is a good place to hear, and possibly see, the canyon tree frog, plus the American dipper and other park wildlife. For additional information, see chapter 4, "Hikes & Other Outdoor Pursuits in Zion National Park," and chapter 10, "A Nature Guide to Zion & Bryce Canyon National Parks."

For a unique hiking experience as well as a close-up look at the power of water, venture into **the Narrows** ★★★, a section of the Virgin River where the canyon walls are less than 30 feet in spots but stand over 1,000 feet tall. To travel between these delicately sculpted rock walls, you'll hike and wade. The Narrows can be experienced as a short day hike, a long 1-day-through hike, or an overnight hike—although caution is needed because the Narrows is prone to flash flooding. For details, see chapter 4, "Hikes & Other Outdoor Pursuits in Zion National Park" and chapter 10, "A Nature Guide to Zion & Bryce Canyon National Parks."

An often-overlooked area of Zion National Park is the **Kolob Canyons** section, in the park's northwest corner. With its narrow canyons and brightly colored cliffs, this is a somewhat different world than Zion Canyon. There's a scenic drive with spectacular overlooks, and several hiking trails. See the section "Seeing the Park by Car and Shuttle," below, as well as chapter 4, "Hikes & Other Outdoor Pursuits in Zion National Park."

Photo Tip

The key to getting good wildlife photos is to know the animals' habits, such as where they go and when. Then, get there first and quietly wait.

Zion Canyon

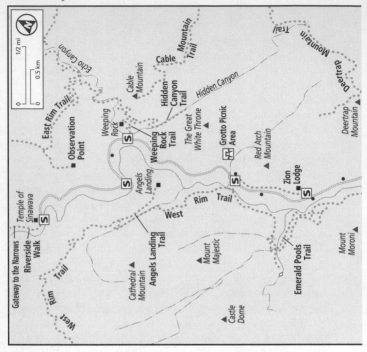

4 How to See the Park in 1 or 2 Days

The best way to see Zion is to spend a week, starting with the visitor center displays and programs, then a Zion Canyon Scenic Drive trip on the shuttle bus, and gradually working from short hikes and walks to full-day and overnight treks into the backcountry. That's the ideal; but for most visitors, time and finances dictate a shorter visit.

If you have only a day or two, we recommend that your first stop be the **Zion Canyon Visitor Center** to see the exhibits, look through the free *Zion Map & Guide,* which describes the available options, and finally talk with a ranger about the amount of time you have, your abilities, and interests. Because Zion has such a variety of landscapes and activities, each visitor can easily create his or her own itinerary.

If your goal is to see as much of the park as possible in 1 full day, we suggest the following:

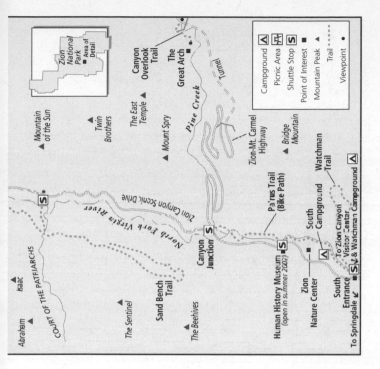

After a quick stop at the visitor center, hop on the shuttle bus, which hits the major Zion Canyon roadside viewpoints. But, when you get to the **Temple of Sinawava,** instead of just taking a quick look and jumping on the next shuttle, hike the easy 2-mile round-trip **Riverside Walk,** which follows the Virgin River through a narrow canyon past hanging gardens. Then continue the shuttle bus trek back to the lodge (total time: 2 to 4 hr.), where you might stop at the gift shop and possibly have lunch in the lodge restaurant.

Near the lodge, you'll find the trail head for the **Emerald Pools.** Especially pleasant on hot days, this easy walk through a forest of oak, maple, fir, and cottonwood trees leads to a waterfall, hanging garden, and the shimmering lower pool. This part of the walk should take about an hour round-trip; those with a bit more ambition may want to add another hour and another mile to the loop by taking the moderately strenuous hike on a rocky, steeper trail to the upper pool.

Wildlife Viewing & Bird Watching

It's a rare visitor to Zion who doesn't spot a critter of some sort, from **mule deer**—often observed along roadways and in campgrounds year-round—to the numerous varieties of lizards seen from spring through fall, including the park's largest lizard, the **chuckwalla,** which can grow to 20 inches long. There has been an increasing number of sightings of **desert bighorn sheep** and even an occasional **mountain lion** along Utah 9 (the Zion–Mt. Carmel Highway) on the east side of the park. Along the Virgin River, you'll see **bank beaver,** so named because they live in burrows dug into riverbanks instead of building dams.

If you're interested in spotting birds, you're in luck at Zion. The **peregrine falcon,** among the world's fastest birds, is sometimes seen along the Angels Landing and Cable Mountain trails and in the area of the Great White Throne. It sometimes nests in the Weeping Rock area, where you're also likely to see the American dipper, canyon wren, and white-throated swift. **Bald eagles** sometimes winter in the park; and you might also see golden eagles. **Red-tailed hawks** are fairly common, plus you're likely to see great blue herons, American kestrels, Gambel's quail, mourning doves, great horned owls, western kingbirds, common ravens, piñon jays, Steller's jays, yellow-rumped warblers, and American robins.

Snakes include the poisonous **Great Basin rattlesnake,** found below 8,000 feet elevation; there are also nonpoisonous king snakes and gopher snakes. Amphibians found in the park include the Arizona tiger salamander, Great Basin spadefoot, red-spotted toad, and northern leopard frog. **Tarantulas,** those large, usually slow-moving hairy spiders, are often seen in late summer and fall. Contrary to popular belief, the tarantula's bite is not significantly poisonous to most people, although it may be somewhat painful.

Remember, it's illegal to feed the wildlife. No matter how much you may want to befriend an animal by offering food, please remember that it's not healthy for the wildlife to eat human food or to get used to being fed this way. For additional details on the wildlife at Zion, see chapter 10, "A Nature Guide to Zion & Bryce Canyon National Parks."

If you still have time and energy, drive back toward the south park entrance and stop at **Watchman Trail Head.** Here, a moderately strenuous, 2-mile, 2-hour round-trip hike takes you to a plateau with beautiful views of several rock formations and the town of Springdale. For details on these trails, see chapter 4, "Hikes & Other Outdoor Pursuits in Zion National Park." That evening, try to take in the campground amphitheater program.

5 Seeing the Park by Car & Shuttle

If you enter the park from the east, along the steep **Zion–Mt. Carmel Highway,** you'll travel 13 miles to the **Zion Canyon Visitor Center,** passing between the White Cliffs and Checkerboard Mesa, a massive sandstone rock formation covered with horizontal and vertical lines that make it look like a huge fishing net. Continuing, you'll pass through a fairyland of fantastically shaped rocks of red, orange, tan, and white, as well as the **Great Arch of Zion,** carved by the forces of erosion high in a stone cliff. At the east end of the Zion–Mt. Carmel Tunnel is the **trail head parking** for the Canyon Overlook Trail, a relatively easy 1-mile walk to a great viewpoint (see chapter 4, "Hikes & Other Outdoor Pursuits in Zion National Park"). After driving through the tunnel (see "Regulations," under "Essentials," earlier in this chapter), you'll traverse a number of long switchbacks as you descend to the canyon floor.

The park's shuttle bus system consists of two loops: one in the town of Springdale and the other along Zion Canyon Scenic Drive, with the loops connecting at the new transit/visitor center just inside the south park entrance. March through October, access to Zion Canyon Scenic Drive (above Utah 9) is limited to shuttle buses, hikers, and bikers. The only exception will be overnight Zion Lodge guests and tour buses connected with the lodge, which will have access as far as the lodge. Shuttle stops are located at all the major-use areas in the park, and shuttles run frequently (about every 6 min. at peak times). In winter, when visitation is lowest in the park, visitors are permitted to drive the full length of Zion Canyon Scenic Drive in their own vehicles. Complete information about the shuttle and all stops is available at the visitor center.

Tip
The earlier in the day you can get out on the Zion Canyon Scenic Drive, the better chance you'll have of seeing wildlife.

The ride through Zion Canyon is impressive by any standards, with massive stone reaching straight up to the heavens, and the North Fork of the Virgin River threading its way through the maze of rocks. In every direction the views are awe-inspiring. Pullouts along the road provide access to viewpoints and hiking trails (see chapter 4, "Hikes & Other Outdoor Pursuits in Zion National Park").

The first pullout is across from the **Court of the Patriarchs,** where a short paved trail leads to an impressive viewpoint. The next stop is **Zion Lodge** (see chapter 5, "Where to Stay, Camp & Eat in Zion"), and across the road from the lodge is the trail head for the **Emerald Pools trail system.** The Grotto Picnic Area is about a half mile beyond the lodge, and a trail, paralleling Zion Canyon Scenic Drive, leads from the lodge to the picnic area. Across from the Grotto Picnic Area parking lot is a footbridge that leads to the Emerald Pools, Angels Landing, and West Rim trails.

Continuing north into Zion Canyon, the road passes the **Great White Throne** on the right and then **Angels Landing** on the left, before the turnoff to the **Weeping Rock Trail Head** parking area. From here the road closely traces the curves of the river, with a couple of stops to allow different views of **the Organ,** which to some resembles a huge pipe organ. Finally the road ends at the **Temple of Sinawava,** where the paved **Riverside Walk** follows the Virgin River toward **the Narrows,** one of the most incredible sights in Zion.

To escape the crowds of Zion Canyon, head to the northwest corner of the park. The **Kolob Canyons Road** (about 45 min. from Zion Canyon Visitor Center at I-15 exit 40) runs 5 miles among spectacular red and orange rocks, ending at a high vista. Allow about 45-minutes round-trip, including stopping at numbered viewpoints. Be sure to get a copy of the Kolob Canyons Road Guide at the Kolob Visitor Center. Here's what you'll pass along the way:

Leaving **Kolob Canyons Visitor Center,** you'll drive along the Hurricane Fault to **Hurricane Cliffs,** a series of tall, gray cliffs composed of limestone, and onward to **Taylor Creek,** where a piñon-juniper forest clings to life on the rocky hillside, providing a home to the bright blue scrub jay. Your next stop is **Horse Ranch Mountain,** which, at 8,726 feet, is the park's highest point. Passing a series of colorful rock layers, where you might be lucky enough to spot a golden eagle, your next stop is **Box Canyon,** along the South Fork of Taylor Creek, with sheer rock walls soaring over 1,500 feet high. Along this stretch you'll see multicolored layers of rock, pushed upward by tremendous forces from within the earth, followed by a side canyon, with large, arched alcoves boasting delicate curved ceilings. Head on to a view of **Timber Top Mountain,** which has a sagebrush-blanketed desert at its base, but is covered with stately fir and ponderosa pine at its peak. Watch for mule deer on the brushy hillsides, especially between October and March, when they might be spotted just after sunrise or before sunset. From here, continue to **Rockfall Overlook;** a large scar on the mountainside marks the spot where a 1,000-foot chunk of stone crashed to the earth in July 1983, the victim of erosion. And finally, stop to see the canyon walls themselves, colored orange-red by iron oxide and striped black by mineral-laden water running down the cliff faces.

Probably the least visited area of the park is between Zion Canyon and Kolob Canyons, accessible via the **Kolob Terrace Road** (also called the Kolob Road). Heading north off Utah 9 from the village of Virgin, about 15 miles west of the park's southern entrance, the Kolob Terrace Road climbs through a piñon juniper woodlands, past grassy meadows, and finally up into a forest of tall ponderosa pines and old stands of aspen. There's a viewpoint offering panoramic vistas across the park, a picnic area, vault toilets, and the small Lava Point Campground. Views from the road are good going up, but more dramatic coming down. This road is closed in the winter.

6 Historic & Man-Made Attractions

There are no major historic sites at Zion National Park, but there is some archaeological evidence of the early peoples who inhabited the area, plus a few 20th-century structures of historic interest. Archaeologists say that evidence has been found throughout the park of several historic and prehistoric cultures. These include people from what is called the **Archaic Period,** who are believed to have occupied the area from about 7,000 to 2,500 years ago; people of the **Virgin Anasazi Pueblo culture,** who are believed to have lived at Zion until about A.D. 1150; and finally the **Southern Paiutes,** who arrived in the area at about A.D. 1100 and stayed until European settlers arrived about 1860. Although there are no designated and marked archaeological sites, hikers with sharp eyes may see pot shards, pieces of ancient stone tools, rock art, and other artifacts. There's one site near the park's south entrance; ask rangers for specific directions. Park officials ask that you **refrain from touching** these artifacts—especially rock art and painted pottery, because skin oils can damage them—and that you not move them.

From the **Weeping Rock** parking area, you can see remains of a **cable operation** that was used to lower millions of board feet of timber from Cable Mountain to the floor of Zion Canyon between 1901 and 1926 (see Cable Mountain and Deertrap Mountain Trails in chapter 4). The timber was used for the building of pioneer settlements along the Virgin River.

Along **Taylor Creek** in the Kolob Canyons section of the park are the remains of two cabins. The **Gustav Larson homestead cabin,** built in 1930 of white fir logs brought from Cedar City, is near the confluence of the North and Middle forks. A **second homestead cabin,** also built of white fir logs in 1930, but by Arthur Fife, a teacher at Southern Utah State college (now Southern Utah University), is perched on a bench above the north bank of the creek (see "Middle Fork of Taylor Creek Trail," in chapter 4).

Also from that period is the **Zion–Mt. Carmel Tunnel,** which you'll drive through if entering or leaving the park on the east side. Dedicated on July 4, 1930, the 1.1-mile tunnel cost over $500,000 and took over 3 years to build. Another historic structure, the handsome **Zion Lodge,** was built in 1925 by the Union Pacific Railroad, but was destroyed by fire in 1966. It was rebuilt the following year and restored to its historic appearance in 1991. Several 1920s-era **tourist cabins** are located near the lodge.

7 Ranger Programs

Park rangers present a variety of free programs and activities. **Amphitheater programs,** which sometimes include a slide show, take place most evenings at campground amphitheaters. Topics vary, but could include the animals or plants of the park, geology, the night sky, mankind's role in the park, or some unique aspect like Zion's slot canyons. Rangers also give **short talks** on similar subjects at various locations, including the Zion Lodge auditorium. Ranger-guided hikes and walks, which may require reservations, might take you to little-visited areas of the park, on a trek to see wildflowers, or for a night hike under a full moon. Schedules of the various activities are posted on bulletin boards at the visitor centers, campgrounds, and other locations.

8 Guided Tours

Guided **horseback rides** in the park are available from Canyon Trail Rides (see chapter 4, "Hikes & Other Outdoor Pursuits in Zion National Park").

Just outside the park, guided hikes are offered by **Bike Zion,** 1458 Zion Park Blvd., Springdale (© **800/4SLIKROK** or

> ## (Kids) Kidding Around
>
> Kids love the huge screen and dramatic photography in the *Zion Canyon—Treasure of the Gods* production at the **Zion Canyon Theatre.** See chapter 9, "Nearby Things to See & Do."

435/772-3929; www.bikezion.com), starting at $35 for a 2½-hour hike or mountain-bike trip, as well as multi-day trips. The company also rents bikes.

Several **national tour operators** offer guided biking, hiking, and backpacking trips in the park area (although not in the park itself—commercial guided hikes are prohibited in Zion), as well as more traditional tours; see "Adventure Vacations & Organized Tours" in chapter 2, "Planning Your Trip to Zion & Bryce Canyon National Parks."

9 Especially for Kids

One of the nicest things about Zion National Park is the wide variety of hiking trails, so there is usually a path suited to every family member's ability level. Among trails that children find especially enjoyable are the **Weeping Rock Trail,** because it leads to a fascinating rock that oozes water; and the various **Emerald Pools trails,** which take you to a series of attractive little pools, where you just might see—or at least hear—some frogs. The only problem at the Emerald Pools is that kids (and adults, too) have to resist the strong urge to submerge their toes in the dark green water.

Older youths—perhaps young teens—who are in good physical condition will enjoy hiking into **the Narrows** from the end of the Riverside Walk, where a hike is almost a swim, and you're staring up from the bottom of a 1,000-foot ravine. However, the Narrows can be very hazardous, so everyone planning to hike it should discuss their plans with park rangers before setting out. See chapter 4, "Hikes & Other Outdoor Pursuits in Zion National Park" for additional hiking information.

Park rangers also have special programs just for children. Kids up to 12 years old can join the **Junior Rangers,** participate in a variety of hands-on activities, and earn certificates, pins, and patches. Morning and afternoon sessions, each lasting 2½ hours, take place daily from Memorial Day to Labor Day, with children meeting at the Nature Center in the South Campground. There's a one-time fee of $2 per child, and the age range is strictly enforced.

Hikes & Other Outdoor Pursuits in Zion National Park

Zion offers a wide variety of hiking trails, ranging from easy half-hour walks to grueling overnight hikes. Several free brochures on hiking trails are available at the visitor centers, and the **Zion Natural History Association** publishes several good booklets describing established trails and off-trail routes (see chapter 2, "Planning Your Trip to Zion & Bryce Canyon National Parks"). Hikers with a fear of heights should be especially careful when choosing trails—many include steep, dizzying drop-offs. Ratings here are provided by the authors and other experienced hikers, and are entirely subjective.

Guided hiking and biking trips in the area outside the park are offered by several local companies, including **Zion Adventure Company,** 36 Lion Blvd. (P.O. Box 523), Springdale, UT 84767 (© **435/772-1001;** fax 435/772-3590; www.zionadventures.com), and **Bike Zion,** 1458 Zion Park Blvd. (P.O. Box 272), Springdale, UT 84767 (© **800/475-4576** or 435/772-3929; www.bikezion.com). National companies offering guided hiking/biking trips in the area are discussed in chapter 2, "Planning Your Trip to Zion & Bryce Canyon National Parks." Shuttle service for backcountry hikers and bikers is available throughout the area from **Zion Canyon Transportation** (© **877/635-5993** or 435/635-5993), which is the only shuttle company authorized to operate within Zion National Park. Those who want to try to arrange rides with fellow hikers can make use of a bulletin board at the visitor center.

1 Day Hikes

Hikers have the chance to see the park from two perspectives—either a high plateau trip that looks down into the canyons, or a descent into the canyons that provides spectacular views skyward.

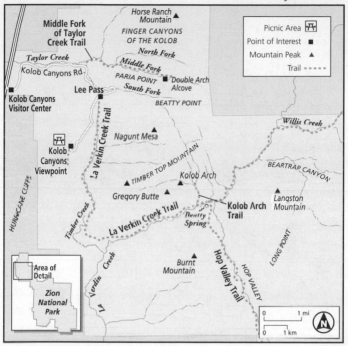

On map:
Horse Ranch Mountain ▲
Middle Fork of Taylor Creek Trail
FINGER CANYONS OF THE KOLOB
North Fork
Taylor Creek
Middle Fork
Kolob Canyons Rd.
PARIA POINT ■ Double Arch
Lee Pass ■ South Fork Alcove
Kolob Canyons Visitor Center ■
BEATTY POINT
Willis Creek
Nagunt Mesa ▲
Kolob Canyons Viewpoint 🏕 ■
TIMBER TOP MOUNTAIN
BEARTRAP CANYON
Timber Creek
Kolob Arch ●
La Verkin Creek Trail
Gregory Butte ▲
Langston Mountain ▲
Kolob Arch Trail
La Verkin Creek Trail
Beatty Spring ○
LONG POINT
HURRICANE CLIFFS
La Verkin Creek
Burnt Mountain ▲
Hop Valley Trail
HOP VALLEY

Legend:
Picnic Area 🏕
Point of Interest ■
Mountain Peak ▲
Trail •••••

Area of Detail
Zion National Park

0   1 mi
0   1 km
N

SHORTER HIKES

Court of the Patriarchs This short, steep, paved hike leads to a viewpoint that provides vistas of the Streaked Wall and the Sentinel to the south, the Court of the Patriarchs and Mount Moroni straight ahead (west), the Spearhead and Angels Landing to the north, and Mountain of the Sun and Twin Brothers above and behind (east). A footbridge crosses the river and connects to the Sand Bench Trail.

100 yards RT. Easy. Access: Court of the Patriarchs parking area along Zion Canyon Scenic Drive.

Weeping Rock Trail 👣👣 *Kids* This is among the park's shortest hikes. A self-guided nature trail, with interpretive signs explaining the natural history of the area, it takes you through a mixed forest to a rock alcove with lush hanging gardens of ferns and wild-flowers. The mist that emanates from the Weeping Rock above is delightfully refreshing on a hot afternoon. Although paved, the trail is relatively steep (gaining 98 ft.) and not suitable for wheelchairs.

0.5 miles RT. Easy to moderate. Access: Weeping Rock parking lot on Zion Canyon Scenic Drive.

Canyon Overlook Trail Panoramic vistas are the lure on this self-guided trail that takes you to an overlook offering a magnificent view of lower Zion Canyon, the East and West temples, the Towers of the Virgin, and the Streaked Wall. The trail, which is sometimes slippery because of sand, begins with a series of uneven steps cut into the sandstone. There are long drop-offs into the narrow chasm of Pine Creek Canyon. It has an elevation gain of 163 feet. Guidebooks are available at the Zion Canyon Visitor Center and at the trailhead.

1 mile RT. Moderate. Access: Parking area at the east terminus of the Zion–Mt. Carmel Tunnel.

Emerald Pools Trail System ★★ *Kids* This can be either an easy 1-hour walk or a moderately strenuous 2-hour hike. A 0.6-mile paved path leads from the Emerald Pools parking area through a forest of oak, maple, fir, and cottonwood, to several waterfalls, a hanging garden, and the picturesque Lower Emerald Pool. From here, a steeper, rocky trail continues a quarter mile to Middle Emerald Pool; and then climbs another 0.3 miles past cactus, yucca, and juniper to Upper Emerald Pool, with another waterfall. As you climb the trail, there are views of soaring stone formations such as Lady Mountain, the Spearhead, Mount Majestic, Red Arch Mountain, Deer Trap Mountain, and the Great White Throne. From the Middle Pool there is a long drop-off leading to the Lower Pool; the Upper Pool is enclosed on three sides by sheer cliffs and on the fourth by boulders. The pools are named for the green color of the water, which is caused by algae. Total elevation gain is 69 feet to Lower Emerald Pool, 150 feet to the middle pool, and 400 feet from the trail head to Upper Emerald Pool. Swimming or wading is not permitted in any of the pools.

1.2–2.5 miles RT. Easy to moderate. Access: Trail head across from Zion Lodge.

Riverside Walk & Gateway to the Narrows ★★★ An easy, paved trail follows the Virgin River upstream to the beginning of the Zion Canyon Narrows, with trailside exhibits and hanging wildflowers in spring and summer. Accessible for people with disabilities with some assistance, the trail has an elevation change of only 57 feet over its 2 miles. The pavement ends at the Narrows, and here you either turn around and head back, or continue upstream into the Narrows, where the canyon walls are sometimes less than 30 feet apart but more than 1,000 feet high. You should have a sturdy hiking staff to help keep your footing as you wade into the cold river over slippery rocks. Before entering the Narrows, check the weather forecast (posted at Zion Canyon Visitor Center) and discuss your plans with park rangers— during rainstorms (common in July and August), flash floods are a serious threat. For more information, see "The Narrows," under "Exploring the Backcountry," later in this chapter.

2 miles RT minimum. Paved and easy. Access: Temple of Sinawava at the end of Zion Canyon Scenic Drive.

Hidden Canyon Trail A particularly scenic hike along a paved trail sometimes cut from solid stone, Hidden Canyon Trail climbs 850 feet to the mouth of a narrow water-carved canyon. You'll pass slickrock formations and sheer cliffs—stay back from the edge as they may be unstable and slippery. Walking up the dry streambed into the canyon, you'll pass grottoes and other water-formed decorations on the canyon walls, including a small natural arch about a half mile upstream from the mouth of the canyon. This trail is not recommended for anyone with a fear of heights.

2 miles RT. Moderate to strenuous. Access: Weeping Rock parking lot along Zion Canyon Scenic Drive.

Watchman Trail 🐾 This moderately strenuous hike gets surprisingly little use, possibly because it can be very hot in the middle of the day. Climbing 368 feet to a plateau near the base of the Watchman formation, it offers splendid views of lower Zion Canyon, Oak Creek Canyon, the Towers of the Virgin, and the West Temple formations. Stay on the main trail created by the National Park Service—it's 3 feet wide—and avoid the smaller crisscross trails created by mule deer seeking water and food. The area traversed by the trail is a spring seepage/riparian area rich with a variety of plants—walk quietly and watch for wildlife, especially birds.

3 miles RT. Moderate. Access: Zion Canyon Visitor Center and Transportation Hub.

West Bank of the Virgin River A pleasant hike along the river, this trail affords views of Zion Canyon plus the opportunity to see a myriad of birds, and an occasional mule deer coming out for a drink in the early evening. After crossing the Virgin River at the Court of the Patriarchs Viewpoint, turn left into the middle of the Court and stop for a moment to gaze up at these awe-inspiring monoliths of stone. Leaving the Court, the trail turns north, levels out, and enters the riparian environment of the river, where you'll be walking amid cottonwood and box elder. As you trek northward, watch for Cathedral Mountain and Mount Majestic to slowly raise their heads above you. This section of the trail is used heavily by horseback-riding groups (see "Horseback Riding," later in this chapter), so be prepared to step aside quietly (and watch where you step).

Once past the spur leading east to Zion Lodge across Zion Canyon Scenic Drive, horse traffic comes to an end, and you embark on the wide, paved trail to the Emerald Pools. Follow the main trail up, around, and down to the Lower Pool, bypassing the spur trails leading to the Upper Pools. Follow signs for the Grotto Trail Head as you leave the Lower Pool, winding through lovely rock gardens and past delightful waterfalls. As the trail angles northward again to follow the river, the Great White Throne gradually emerges into view across the river; cross the bridge to the Grotto Trail Head.

2.6 miles one-way. Easy. Access: Court of the Patriarchs Viewpoint at the south end, the Grotto Trail Head at the north end, both along Zion Canyon Scenic Drive.

Sand Bench Trail This trail is most popular with hikers in the off-season, since horseback riders use it heavily April through October. After crossing the river on the footbridge, this sandy trail turns left and meanders through a sagebrush meadow in the Court of the Patriarchs. It's not always well marked, so watch carefully for the junction where you'll take the left fork across a small streambed, after which the 500-foot climb to the top of the bench begins. Soon the loop splits; if you choose the right fork, you'll pass under sheer stone walls and stark towers until you come out on top, where the Streaked Wall dominates the near view and the Watchman stands sentinel in the distance. As you approach the base of the Streaked Wall, you'll come to a rest area and corral that mark the end of the loop. The trail back takes you along the edge of an escarpment above the river, offering magnificent views of the Twin Brothers, Mountain of the Sun, and East Temple. Remember, horses have the right-of-way, so step to the side of the trail and stand quietly while they pass.

3.4-mile loop. Moderate. Access: Court of the Patriarchs Viewpoint along Zion Canyon Scenic Drive.

Pa'rus Trail 🚶🚶 *Kids*   This easy, paved trail (suitable for wheelchairs and baby strollers) follows the Virgin River, crossing it several times. It provides views of the rock formations in lower Zion Canyon, including the West Temple, Watchman, Bridge Mountain, Sentinel, and East Temple formations. The trail has a 50-foot elevation gain and, unlike other park trails, is also open to bicycles (see "Biking & Mountain Biking," later in this chapter) and leashed pets. Watch for stop signs where the trail crosses park roads, stay alert, and be aware of vehicles whose drivers may not easily see you on the winding roads. This trail links the campgrounds and south park entrance with the beginning of Zion Canyon Scenic Drive (now closed to private vehicles), and the rest of Zion Canyon.

3.5 miles RT. Easy. Access: Either the entrance to Watchman Campground, near the amphitheater parking area; or near the Nature Center in South Campground.

Angels Landing Trail 🚶🚶   A popular though strenuous hike that is most certainly not for anyone with even a mild fear of heights, this trail climbs 1,488 feet to a summit that offers spectacular views into Zion Canyon. But be prepared: The final half mile follows a narrow, knife-edge trail along a steep ridge, where footing can be slippery even under the best of circumstances.

After crossing the footbridge over the Virgin River, turn north through a riparian woodland of cottonwood, box elder, and tamarisk, above which Angels Landing beckons. The trail climbs to the mouth of Refrigerator Canyon around the west side of the monolith. Grottos and overhangs dot the red sandstone canyon walls. Shortly before reaching the head of the canyon, a series of 21 switchbacks have been built into a cleft in the wall; they are regarded as one of the engineering marvels of the park. At the top of the switchbacks, you begin the gradual ascent to Scout Lookout, the saddle behind Angels Landing from which you get spectacular views into Zion Canyon.

Here also, the West Rim Trail heads off to the left, while the Angels Landing Trail turns southeast and begins the final brutal climb along the spine of a razorlike ridge. From this point, many stretches have support chains to hold on to, but there are no guardrails on Angels Landing itself. But the views are stupendous, with the Virgin River gently bending around three sides at the bottom of the canyon, the Great White Throne and Red Arch Mountain to the southeast, and the entrance to the Narrows beyond the Temple of Sinawava to the north.

5 miles RT. Difficult. Access: Grotto Picnic Area along Zion Canyon Scenic Drive.

Middle Fork of Taylor Creek Trail   You will probably get your feet wet as you hike along Taylor Creek and its Middle Fork, fording it several times. Following the creek bed upstream, you'll have views of Tucupit and Paria Points directly ahead and Horse Ranch Mountain to the left. The Gustav Larson cabin is near the confluence of the North and Middle forks, after which the trail begins its ascent into the canyon between Tucupit and Paria points; it levels out as it follows the creek bed. A second homestead cabin is perched on a bench above the north bank of the creek (see "Historic & Man-Made Attractions," in chapter 3). The trail ends at Double Arch Alcove, a large colorful grotto with the arch high above. The term alcove denotes an arch against rock, with no space for light to pass through. The trail has an elevation gain of 450 feet.

5.4 miles RT. Moderately strenuous. Access: Trail head parking area along Kolob Canyons Rd., about 2 miles from Kolob Canyons Visitor Center.

LONGER HIKES

East Mesa Trail 🏇   This is an easier and shorter route to Observation Point than the Observation Point Trail (see below), and is open to equestrians. The trail heads westward over a fairly open plateau through ponderosa pines and manzanita, turning a little to the south as it passes Mystery Canyon, winds around a steep unnamed canyon opening to the south into Echo Canyon, and then passes another canyon to the north that empties into the Virgin River just below the Narrows. Finally the trail connects to Observation Point Trail just 0.2 miles from its end; turn right for Observation Point.

6 miles RT. Easy. Access: E. Mesa Trail Head. (From Zion National Park's east entrance drive 2.4 miles east on Utah 9, turn north onto the road to the North Fork and Navajo Lake—impassable when wet or snowy—and go 5.3 miles to the Ponderosa Hunting Club. Visitors should register at the small mailbox at the Ponderosa Gate—sign both in and out. Drive through the main entrance and head left [west] on Twin Knolls Rd. for about 1.2 miles to a T intersection; turn right [north] onto Beaver Rd., which deteriorates into little more than a dirt track and eventually re-enters the park at the trailhead.)

Cable Mountain and Deertrap Mountain Trails   From the Ponderosa Hunting Club Trail Head, you'll head west into an open ponderosa pine forest, which soon gives way to a meadow of sagebrush, where you join the East Rim Trail (see below). A trail to Echo Canyon heads off to the right; take the left fork for Cable and Deertrap mountains. At the next fork, your route bears right and the East Rim Trail veers left. The trail climbs through juniper, piñon, Gambel oak, and a few ponderosa pines, then tops out in

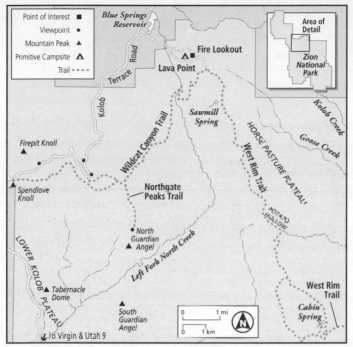

Map legend:
- Point of Interest ■
- Viewpoint •
- Mountain Peak ▲
- Primitive Campsite △
- Trail ••••

Area of Detail — Zion National Park

Blue Springs Reservoir
Fire Lookout
Lava Point
Kolob Terrace Road
Sawmill Spring
Wildcat Canyon Trail
Kolob Creek
Goose Creek
Firepit Knoll
Spendlove Knoll
Northgate Peaks Trail
HORSE PASTURE PLATEAU
West Rim Trail
POTATO HOLLOW
North Guardian Angel
Left Fork North Creek
LOWER KOLOB PLATEAU
Tabernacle Dome
South Guardian Angel
West Rim Trail
Cabin Spring
To Virgin & Utah 9

0   1 mi
0   1 km

N

open sagebrush. Here the trail separates, the right branch for Cable Mountain and the left for Deertrap Mountain.

The **Cable Mountain Trail** climbs gently to a knoll from which you can see the more than 10,000-foot-high pink cliffs of the Virgin Rim in the distance, before descending into a manzanita and juniper forest. The trail gradually makes its way northwest along a plateau to the point where pioneers built a cable tramway to carry logs down to the Virgin River (see "Historic & Man-Made Attractions," in chapter 3). The remains of the tram structure are fragile and very hazardous—please stay back. Looking out over the Big Bend of the Virgin River you have a grand view of the Organ and Angels Landing with the cliffs of Cathedral Mountain serving as a backdrop. This trail has an elevation gain of 530 feet and a loss of 460 feet.

The **Deertrap Mountain Trail** slopes downward from the junction with Cable Mountain Trail toward the head of Hidden Canyon. As you cross an open area dotted with manzanita, several paths lead to the bottom of a draw where there's a small seep. Follow the trail out onto Deertrap Mountain and to the rim of Zion Canyon for a breathtaking view of the Mountain of the Sun and the Twin Brothers practically in your lap, and the Court of the Patriarchs directly across the canyon. From here, you can walk north and south along the edge of the canyon. The better-defined path runs north (0.4 miles) to an overlook from which you can see the Great White Throne, Angels Landing, and in the distance the red tips of the Temple of Sinawava. The southern path (0.6 miles) is rough, and leads to a view of the East Temple and Twin Brothers. This trail has an elevation gain of 760 feet and a loss of 470 feet.

These hikes can also be done as an overnight trip from the Ponderosa Hunting Club Trail Head; or for the really zealous, there's the option of combining these with the more strenuous East Rim Trail (see below), which adds 11.2 miles to the jaunt.

6.2 miles RT to Cable Mountain, 7.8 miles RT to Deertrap Mountain, or 10.9 miles combination RT. Moderate. Access: Ponderosa Hunting Club. (From Zion National Park's east entrance drive 2.4 miles east on Utah 9, turn north onto the road to the North Fork and Navajo Lake—impassable when wet or snowy—for 5.3 miles to the Ponderosa Hunting Club. Visitors should register at the small mailbox at the Ponderosa Gate—sign both in and out. Drive through the main entrance and head left [west] on Twin Knolls Rd. for about 0.8 miles; turn left [south] onto Buck Rd. Bear right at the first Y, then left at the next Y, following signs for the Gooder-Reagan cabin. The last few hundred yards descends a rocky grade and crosses a wash, requiring a high-clearance vehicle, before entering the national park at the trail head. Close the gate behind you to keep livestock out.)

Observation Point Trail   This hike climbs over 2,000 feet to Observation Point, but the incredible views make all the exertion worthwhile. As you climb the switchbacks zigzagging up the canyon wall, a variety of formations become visible. First there's Angels Landing across the Virgin River and the Organ a little closer, then the alcove containing Weeping Rock to the north. Cathedral Mountain appears from beyond Angels Landing, and the sheer north face of Cable Mountain looms directly overhead. The trail levels out as it enters Echo Canyon. When the East Rim Trail branches off to the right you head left up the north wall of Echo Canyon, climbing along steep switchbacks until the trail heads across a steep slope of white cliffs dropping 1,000 feet below the path. When you finally reach the top of the Navajo sandstone formation, the East Mesa Trail heads off to the right and you bend around to the left through deep sand to Observation Point, right at the tip of the plateau, at an altitude of 6,507 feet. From here you can see far down Zion Canyon; the Great White Throne looms in the foreground with Red Arch Mountain just beyond. For an easier hike to Observation Point, take the East Mesa Trail (see above).

8 miles RT. Moderately strenuous. Access: Weeping Rock parking lot along Zion Canyon Scenic Drive.

East Rim Trail   Your exertions will be rewarded with a variety of views on this challenging trail, which connects with the trails to Cable and Deertrap mountains, Observation Point, and Hidden Canyon (see trail descriptions above), before descending into Zion Canyon at the Weeping Rock Trail Head. Trail intersections are fairly well marked all along the East Rim.

The trail follows an old dirt road up the dry wash of Clear Creek and then begins a climb of about 800 feet up the narrow canyon of Cave Creek. Once on top you'll follow the rim high above Clear Creek, providing terrific views of Checkerboard Mesa. At the head of Jolley Gulch you'll find yourself at a high pour-off, looking down at water-smoothed canyon walls. Leaving the rim, the trail winds along the East Rim Plateau, through scattered piñon and Utah juniper, manzanita, and an occasional Gambel oak in wetter areas. This plateau was heavily logged in the early part of the 20th century (see "Cable Mountain and Deertrap Mountain Trails," above). About 5.3 miles along the trail you come to a short spur trail over to Stave Spring, a fairly dependable water source (treat before use). Soon the trail to Cable and Deertrap mountains branches off to the left, and after another half mile the turnoff to the Ponderosa Hunting Club heads right. The East Rim Trail descends toward Echo Canyon, following the top of canyon walls for about a half mile before switch-backing down the almost sheer cliffs into Echo Canyon, and offering views of Cathedral Mountain and Angels Landing. The trail becomes a mite dicey along here, with twists and turns complicated by slickrock where the only trail pointers are rock cairns. But finally you reach the junction with the steep Observation Point Trail, which takes off to the right and once on top connects to the East Mesa Trail (see above). Continuing down Echo Canyon brings you to the end of the trail at Weeping Rock Trail Head, located in Zion Canyon along Zion Canyon Scenic Drive.

10.5 miles one-way to Weeping Rock Trail Head. Difficult. Access: Trail head is at the end of a short paved road past a ranger's residence, 150 yd. west of the east entrance to the park.

Chinle Trail The first few miles of this quiet desert trail are fairly easy walking along a wide sandy path. Ahead you have views of Mount Kinesava and the Three Marys, and behind are the Eagle Crags. A gradual 150-foot incline brings you to the Petrified Forest. (Please remember it is illegal to remove anything from the national park; leave the lovely pieces of petrified wood as you find them.) After crossing Huber Wash the trail heads for Scoggins Wash through more desert terrain, with the addition of juniper, piñon, and sagebrush. To the northwest you can see Cougar Mountain, and looking east allows views of the Towers of the Virgin, the West Temple, and the Sundial. Once on the mesa beyond Scoggins Wash, the trail heads for three knolls, passing through several small saddles, traversing a meadow, and crossing the Old Scoggins Stock Trail, built by the area's early pioneers. Continuing west, the trail passes between two knolls and bends around to the north, where you'll have no trouble finding an attractive campsite. The final descent into Coalpits Wash brings Cougar Mountain, Smith Mesa, and Lambs Knoll into view, and at the bottom you'll have a delightful sight of a pretty waterfall a bit upstream from Coalpits Spring—the end of the trail. This trail can be uncomfortably hot in summer, but an absolute delight November through May, with blankets of wild-flowers to delight the eye in spring. The elevation gain of this hike is a gradual 550 feet over the first 5 miles, after which you drop about 250 feet over the last 3 miles.

16.2 miles RT. Easy to moderate. Access: From the south entrance to the park, drive west on Utah 9 for 3.5 miles to a parking area on the right (north) side of the road. From here, follow a marked trail 1.4 miles through a recent real estate development.

Wildcat Canyon and Wildcat Canyon Connecting Trails A high-country trail linking the Hop Valley and West Rim trails (see "Exploring the Backcountry," below), this connector also provides access to several primitive canyon trails. The Wildcat Trail cuts east (right) just a short distance from the Hop Valley Trail Head, passing between Spendlove Knoll to the south and Firepit Knoll to the north, both extinct cinder cones. Crossing the upper end of the Lee Valley takes you through open grassy meadows sprinkled with sagebrush and Gambel oak. Vistas to the east and south include Northgate Peaks, the tops of North and South Guardian Angels above a reddish ridge, the Altar of Sacrifice, the West Temple, and Mount Kinesava. Cedar posts mark the trail as it becomes obscure in places through the valley, and after crossing the Pine Springs Wash, rock cairns point the way along an incline of slickrock.

As you reach the top of the incline you have a grand unobstructed view of North Guardian Angel. Once past the junctions with spurs to **Wildcat Canyon Trailhead** and **Northgate Peaks Trail** (the first heads left, the second right—continue straight ahead at both), you begin a gentle incline through a ponderosa pine forest continuing upward along Russell Gulch. As you enter the headwaters of Wildcat Canyon you'll see Gambel oak, bigtooth maple, and quaking aspen. In autumn, their wildly colorful displays contrast with the White Cliffs extending to the south and the dark strip of lava across the top of the canyon. The trail descends into the canyon, passing a dependable spring (treat the water before using), and then climbs the far wall, eventually reaching the top of the Horse Pasture Plateau. Just before the junction with the West Rim Trail, you'll have fine views of the Lava Point lookout. At the **West Rim Trail,** turn left to reach **Lava Point Trailhead,** the end of the trail. This trail has a total elevation gain of about 1,500 feet, with numerous ups and downs along the way.

8.7 miles, Hop Valley Trail Head to Lava Point Trail Head. Moderate. Access: From Virgin, head north on Kolob Terrace Rd. about 13 miles to the parking area for Hop Valley Trail Head.

2 Exploring the Backcountry

There are backpacking opportunities galore here, and several of the day hikes discussed above can be more comfortably done in 2 or more days. In addition to the park's established trails and the famous Narrows, there are a number of off-trail routes for those experienced in the use of compasses and topographic maps—get information at the Zion Canyon Visitor Center. Backcountry permits ($5) are required for all overnight hikes in the park as well as slot canyon routes. Backcountry camping is not permitted within 1 mile of a road or trail head.

Hop Valley Trail   This trail loses about 1,000 feet as it meanders northwest through sunny fields and past Gambel oak, partly following an old Jeep road and then a stream, before arriving at La Verkin Creek. Many hikers continue on the La Verkin Creek/Kolob Arch trails to see Kolob Arch.

The beginning of the trail takes you through some rather deep sand, so if your gear includes gaiters, wear them. After passing through the hiker gate in the fence marking the beginning of an inholding (privately owned property within the park), you'll be sharing space with cattle spring through fall. Follow the four-wheel-drive road, marked by fence posts when it becomes almost too faint to see, until you reach the stream in the bottom of the Hop Valley. Follow the stream or cattle trails along it down the valley, and shortly Langston Canyon will come in from the right, sometimes contributing a trickle of water to the stream. About a half mile farther, another fence marks the end of the inholding and the stream sinks into the sand and disappears in summer. A sign marks where the trail leaves the wash and climbs a hill, after which the trail follows a steep descent into the valley of La Verkin Creek. Camping is allowed outside the inholding, and shady sites can be found among the pines not far from the wash. From here you can head to Kolob Arch, about three-quarters of a mile away, explore the La Verkin Creek system, or return to the Hop Valley Trail Head. If you see any cattle outside the inholding, notify the Park Service when you finish your hike.

13.4 miles RT. Moderate to difficult. Access: Trail head on Kolob Terrace Rd., about 13 miles north of Virgin.

La Verkin Creek/Kolob Arch Trails ⟨⟨   La Verkin Creek and its tributaries are responsible for the magnificent canyons cut into the red Navajo sandstone in this section of the park. The hike passes through dry sagebrush flats and forests of conifers, cottonwoods, and box elders; and where water seeps from the stone, hanging gardens astonish the eye. The trail is popular and can be quite busy on summer weekends, in spite of the almost 800-foot net elevation gain of the return trek. From the trail head, you descend to Timber Creek, which is often dry by late summer. Follow it upstream around the base of Shuntavi Butte, Timber Top Mountain, and Gregory Butte; as you climb into a small open bowl, the views widen to the south and east. Soon you'll come to an old corral built by Mormon pioneers, after which there is a short side hike downstream to a series of pretty, though short, waterfalls. Follow La Verkin Creek upstream along the north bank, with Gregory Butte towering overhead on your left and Neagle Ridge jutting up on the right.

When you reach the turnoff to the Kolob Arch Viewpoint, turn left along a tiny tributary with some steep ups-and-downs on rocky footing for about a half mile. Then look up—Kolob Arch soars high overhead about a quarter mile away. One of the largest arches in the world, it measures over 300 feet wide. *Caution:* Going beyond the viewpoint is not recommended due to the instability of the slopes. Back on the main trail a short way upstream, cross over to Beatty

Spring, after which is the junction with **Hop Valley Trail** (heading southeast). You've come about 7 miles and descended to 5,200 feet elevation. Further exploration upstream takes you to Beartrap Canyon and then up Willis Creek, another 4.5 miles with a further elevation loss of just under 200 feet.

14 miles RT. Moderate heading east, strenuous returning west. Access: Kolob Canyons Rd. at Lee Pass.

The Narrows ⋒⋒⋒   Hiking the Narrows is not really hiking a trail at all, but more like wading along the bottom of the North Fork of the Virgin River, through a spectacular 1,000-foot-deep chasm that, at less than 30 feet wide in spots, fulfills its name admirably. Passing fancifully sculptured sandstone arches, hanging gardens, and waterfalls, this hike is recommended for those in good physical condition who are up to fighting sometimes-strong currents. Those who want just a taste of the Narrows can walk and wade in from the other end, from the **Riverside Walk** (see information earlier in this chapter).

The full trip through the Narrows involves a long-day or preferably 2-day trek, which entails arranging a shuttle to the trail head and then transportation from the Temple of Sinawava, where you leave the canyon. From the trail head, on private land, you'll ford the river and follow a dirt road downstream. Please remain on the road and leave all gates as found. The road ends a short distance beyond an old cabin, and from here you will hike either along or in the river, which has cut a deep canyon into the Navajo sandstone. Occasionally you might note a lone conifer leaning out from the stone wall at an absurd angle. Finally the walls are broken only by an occasional steeply ridged canyon created over millennia by some seemingly insignificant stream in its quest to reach the Virgin River. At one point you'll come up against a 12-foot waterfall, where a path circumnavigates this natural barrier by leading you through a slot in the rock.

You are now within the boundary of the park, and in another mile and a half will reach the confluence with Deep Creek, where the canyon widens to absorb this sizable flow of water. In the next 2 miles lie the designated—and assigned—campsites. The current is faster due to the increased flow of water, and the rocks underfoot are slippery, so step carefully to avoid injury. Kolob Creek is the next tributary seen, though it flows only when waters are released from Kolob Reservoir for irrigation downstream; Goose Creek comes in next and signals a deepening of the water—waist-high in some places—and increased speed of the flow. Soon you'll see Big Springs gushing over moss-covered stone on the right wall of the canyon, signifying the beginning of the Narrows.

For the next 3 miles there is no place to climb out of the water in the event of a flash flood, and there is practically no vegetation to grab onto, as any small seedling is periodically ripped from its hold by raging waters. (See the box "The Narrows: Safety First," below.) The river spreads from wall to wall, requiring constant wading in a deep canyon with little light. The water has even undercut the walls near the confluence with Orderville Canyon. Runoff from above oozes from the canyon walls here, providing moisture for hanging gardens and habitat for the minuscule Zion snail, found nowhere else in the world (see chapter 10, "A Nature Guide to Zion & Bryce Canyon National Parks"). About a mile farther where the canyon opens out, a narrow ribbon of water slips out of Mystery Canyon above and skims down the rounded canyon wall. Just beyond, you can finally climb out of the water onto the paved **Riverside Walk** that takes you to the Temple of Sinawava and the end of the hike.

Permits ($5) are required for full-day and overnight hikes originating from Chamberlain's Ranch, which must be purchased at the Zion Canyon Visitor Center the day before your hike; campsites are assigned and the number of hikers, both day and overnight, is limited. Short day hikes, starting and ending at the end of the Riverside Walk, do not require permits.

16 miles one-way. Difficult. Permit required. Access: Chamberlain's Ranch (outside the park); arrange a shuttle for delivery and pickup; see the introduction to this chapter for shuttle information. (From Zion National Park's east entrance drive 2.4 miles east on Utah 9, turn north onto the road to the North Fork and Navajo Lake—impassable when wet or snowy—and go 18 miles. Immediately after crossing the bridge over the Virgin River, turn left onto a gravel road and go 1 mile to the trail head, which is just before the river ford.)

West Rim Trail ⚑   This trail has a net elevation loss of 3,560 feet over 14.2 miles to the Grotto Picnic Area, and many hikers choose to arrange for a shuttle at one end or the other rather than attempting the strenuous climb back to Lava Point—most of the rise is achieved in the first 6 miles from the south end.

Over half of this very popular hike is spent atop the Horse Pasture Plateau, a finger of land pointing toward Angels Landing, which affords incredible vistas all along the trail. The plateau boasts a wide range of plant life and consequently a fascinating variety of birds and animals. The number of blackened hulks of trees attest to the many lightning strikes that have occurred here. Stark reminders

Tips The Narrows: Safety First

Hiking in the Narrows, which are subject to flash flooding, can be treacherous, since there are many sections where there is no place to escape a rushing wall of water. Hiking here is not advised when rain is forecast or threatening; park officials strongly recommend that hikers check the latest National Weather Service forecast before setting out, even when skies appear clear. Weather forecasts are posted at the Zion Canyon Visitor Center, and rangers are available to discuss current conditions, but park officials emphasize that all hikers are responsible for their own safety.

Even those planning just a short day hike into the Narrows, entering from the end of the Riverside Walk, need to spend some time on preparation. Hikers should wear sturdy boots or shoes with good ankle support that they won't mind getting wet; carry an empty bag to pack out all trash; take drinking water, sunscreen, and a first-aid kit; be prepared for cold temperatures with a sweater or jacket; and put everything in waterproof containers.

Experienced Narrows hikers also recommend that you take a walking stick to help steady yourself against the strong currents; sticks are usually available near the end of the Riverside Walk, and hikers should not cut tree branches. Because there are no restrooms in the Narrows, hikers should use the restroom at the Riverside Walk Trail Head before heading out. Park officials request that human waste be buried as far away from the river and other water sources as possible.

Because of strong currents and deep pools, park officials recommend that children under 4'8" tall not hike in the river.

of a wildfire in 1980 can also be seen, and the results of more recent fires display man's increased knowledge of the benefits of monitored and prescribed burns.

At the southern end of the plateau, you can choose to take the **Telephone Canyon Trail** or stay on the Rim Route; the first is a little shorter and they come together again at West Rim Spring

Junction, just before the steep descent into Zion Canyon. The climb down takes you around and behind Mount Majestic and Cathedral Mountain, following part of Refrigerator Canyon, and connects to **Angels Landing Trail** before depositing you at the bridge over the Virgin River near the Grotto Picnic Area.

28.4 miles RT. Difficult. Access: Lava Point Trail Head. (From Virgin, take Kolob Terrace Rd. north about 21 miles, turn right toward Lava Point, and after about a mile there's a fork: If it's dry, take the left fork and drive about 1.3 miles to the trail head; otherwise, take the right fork to Lava Point Campground, where there's a connecting trail to the trail head.)

3 Biking & Mountain Biking

Although bikes are prohibited on almost all trails, as well as forbidden to travel cross-country within the national park boundaries, Zion is among the West's most bike-friendly national parks. The **Pa'rus Trail** runs a little under 2 miles along the Virgin River, from the south park entrance and South Campground to Zion Canyon Scenic Drive, crossing the river and several creeks, and providing good views of the Watchman, West Temple, the Sentinel, and other lower-canyon formations. The trail is paved and open to bicyclists, pedestrians, pets on leashes, and those with strollers or wheelchairs, but is closed to cars.

The **Zion Canyon Scenic Drive,** beyond its intersection with the Zion–Mt. Carmel Highway, is closed to private motor vehicles, except to motorists with reservations at Zion Lodge, April through October. However, the road is open to hikers and bicyclists, as well as shuttle buses.

Bicycles can also be ridden on other park roads, but not through the Zion–Mt. Carmel Tunnel.

Although mountain bikes are prohibited on the trails of Zion National Park (except the Pa'rus Trail), just outside the park— mostly on Bureau of Land Management and state-owned property—are numerous rugged Jeep trails that are great for mountain biking, plus more than 100 miles of slickrock cross-country trails

---

⎛Tips⎞ Bikers Beware

If you have a bike rack on the rear bumper of your car, make sure the bike tires are far from the exhaust pipe; an owner of one bike shop says he does a good business replacing exhaust-cooked bike tires.

---

and single-track trails. **Gooseberry Mesa,** above the community of Springdale, is generally considered the best mountain-biking destination in the area, but there are also good trails on nearby **Grafton Mesa.**

Talk with the knowledgeable staff at **Bike Zion** (see the beginning of this chapter) about the best trails for your interests and abilities. This full-service bike shop also offers maps, a full range of bikes and accessories, repairs, and rentals ($23 to $35 for a full day, $17 to $27 for a half day). Bike Zion also offers guided mountain bike trips outside the park, starting at $35 for a 2½-hour tour, and a variety of multi-day excursions, including some with catered gourmet meals or educational themes.

4 Other Sports & Activities

FISHING   Though not the most popular pastime in the park, fishing in the Virgin River is permitted, with a valid Utah fishing license. Anglers occasionally catch a few trout, but the stream is not stocked.

HORSEBACK RIDING   Horseback riding is permitted in many areas of the park—it's especially popular in the Kolob Canyons section—although it is prohibited on some of the more popular hiking trails. Backcountry permits ($5) are required for overnight trips into the backcountry. For complete details, contact the visitor centers or park offices (see chapter 2, "Planning Your Trip to Zion & Bryce Canyon National Parks") and ask for a copy of the free handout "Pack Animal Use."

Guided rides in the park are available March through October from **Canyon Trail Rides,** P.O. Box 128, Tropic, UT 84776 (© **435/679-8665;** www.onpages.com/canyonrides), with ticket sales and information at Zion Lodge. A 1-hour ride along the Virgin River costs $20 and a half-day ride on the Sand Beach Trail costs $45. Riders must weigh no more than 220 pounds, and children must be at least 5 years old for the 1-hour ride and 8 years old for the half-day ride. Reservations are advised.

ROCK CLIMBING   Expert technical rock climbers like the tall sandstone cliffs in Zion Canyon, although rangers warn that much of the rock is loose, or "rotten," and climbing equipment and techniques suitable for granite are often less effective (and therefore less safe) on sandstone. Permits ($5) are required for overnight climbs, and because some routes may be closed at times, such as during peregrine falcon nesting from early spring through July, climbers should check at the Zion Canyon Visitor Center before setting out. A variety of rock climbing workshops and clinics are offered near the park on public and private land by **Zion Adventure Company** (see beginning of this chapter), with rates starting at about $100 per person (for two or three people) for an 8-hour clinic.

Climbers without the necessary expertise for Zion are advised to try nearby Snow Canyon State Park (see chapter 9, "Nearby Things to See & Do").

SWIMMING & TUBING   Hikers in the Narrows soon find that they are participating in a water sport, as they wade along the "trail" at the bottom of the Virgin River. Tubing and wading are also permitted in other sections of the river—there is a designated river-access area just south of the South Campground amphitheater—but those going into the water should wear shoes to protect their feet. Swimming and wading are prohibited in the Emerald Pools.

WINTER ACTIVITIES   Zion does not usually get enough snow for winter sports, but the relatively warm winter days can be perfect for hiking. However, winter hikers need to be especially careful when trails are icy.

5

Where to Stay, Camp & Eat in Zion

Lodging, dining, and camping choices inside the park are limited to Zion Lodge and the three National Park Service campgrounds, which are wonderful and very much the experience we prefer in a national park vacation. However, you'll probably be heading to the nearby gateway communities for at least some of your dining and lodging, and possibly camping. Generally, the further you get from the park entrances, the less expensive your lodging will be, and outside the park you'll find choices to please almost every taste.

1 Where to Stay

Pets are not accepted unless otherwise noted.

INSIDE THE PARK

Room tax is about 9%.

Zion Lodge ★★★ This handsome lodge was built in 1925 by the Union Pacific Railroad, destroyed by fire in 1966, rebuilt the following year, and then restored to its historic appearance in 1991. The only lodging within the park boundaries, Zion Lodge offers several choices for type of accommodation. Situated in a valley with spectacular views of the park's rock cliffs, the charming and genuinely historic cabins are our choice here because they seem to perfectly fit the national park ambience. Each cabin has a private porch, stone (gas-burning) fireplace, two double beds, and pine board walls. The comfortable motel units are fine for those who prefer more modern accommodations, with one or two queen-size beds and all the usual amenities except televisions. Each has a private balcony. The motel suites, very plush and spacious, have one king-size bed, a separate sitting room with a queen-size hide-a-bed, and a refrigerator.

Ranger programs are offered in the lodge auditorium. A gift shop sells everything from postcards and T-shirts to top quality silver-and-turquoise American Indian jewelry. The lodge fills quickly during the summer, so make reservations as far in advance as possible.

Zion National Park, UT. © **435/772-3213.** Fax 435/772-2001. Information and reservations: Amfac Parks & Resorts, 14001 E. Iliff Ave., Suite 600, Aurora, CO 80014. © **303/297-2757.** Fax 303/297-3175. www.zionlodge.com. 121 units. Motel rooms $97–$117 double; $127–$147 suites; $107–$127 cabins. Discounts and packages available in winter. AE, DISC, MC, V. **Amenities:** Restaurant (see "Where to Eat," later in this chapter). *In room:* A/C.

OUTSIDE THE PARK

Room tax is about 10%. See chapter 9, "Nearby Things to See & Do," for a discussion of things to see and do in these gateway communities.

SPRINGDALE & VIRGIN

For additional information about the area contact the **Zion Canyon Chamber of Commerce,** P.O. Box 331, Springdale, UT 84767-0331 (© **888/518-7070;** www.zionpark.com); or **Utah's Southwest Color Country,** P.O. Box 1550, St. George, UT 84771-1550 (© **800/233-8824** or 435/628-4171; fax 435/673-3540; www.colorcountry.org).

Best Western Zion Park Inn ✿   This is a good choice for those who seek an upscale, reliable, chain motel, with no surprises. Rooms in the handsome two-story complex are tastefully appointed in Southwest style, with two double beds, two queens, or one king-size bed. The grounds are beautifully landscaped, with phenomenal views of the area's red rock formations.

1215 Zion Park Blvd. (P.O. Box 800), Springdale, UT 84767. © **800/934-7275** or 435/772-3200. Fax 435/772-2449. www.zionparkinn.com. 120 units. Apr–Oct $89–$105 double, $115–$160 suite or family unit; Nov–Mar $60–$72 double, $85–$125 suite or family unit. AE, DC, DISC, MC, V. Pets accepted, for an extra fee, with management approval. **Amenities:** Restaurant (American); heated outdoor swimming pool (open Apr–Oct); hot tub; convenience store; liquor store; coin-op laundry. *In room:* A/C, TV, coffeemaker, hair dryer, iron and ironing boards.

Canyon Ranch Motel   Consisting of a series of two- and four-unit cottages set back from the highway, this motel has the look of 1930s-style cabins on the outside while providing modern motel rooms inside. Rooms are either new or newly remodeled, and options include one queen- or king-size bed, two queens, or one queen and one double. Some rooms have showers only, while others have shower/tub combos. Room 13, with two queen-size beds, offers spectacular views of the Zion National Park rock formations

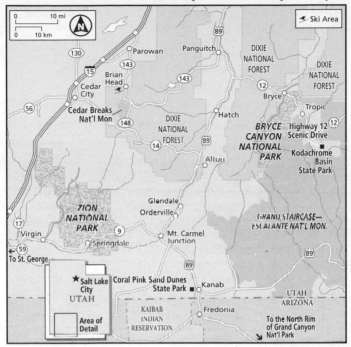

through its large picture windows; views from most other rooms are almost as good. The units surround a lawn with trees and picnic tables.

668 Zion Park Blvd. (P.O. Box 175), Springdale, UT 84767 (**℡ 435/772-3357**, Fax 435/772-3057. www.canyonranchmotel.com. 21 units. Rates per room (up to 5 people): Apr–Oct $58–$88; Nov–Mar $44–$54. AE, DISC, MC, V. Pets accepted at management discretion ($5 per pet per night). **Amenities:** Outdoor pool; whirlpool. *In room:* A/C, TV, some kitchen units available.

Cliffrose Lodge & Gardens *ℛ*   With river frontage and 5 acres of lawns, shade trees, and flower gardens, the Cliffrose offers a beautiful setting just outside the entrance to Zion National Park. The modern, well-kept rooms have all the standard motel appointments, with unusually large bathrooms with shower/tub combinations. On the lawns, you'll find comfortable seating, including a lawn swing.

281 Zion Park Blvd. (P.O. Box 510), Springdale, UT 84767. (**℡ 800/243-UTAH** or 435/772-3234. Fax 435/772-3900. www.cliffroselodge.com. 36 units. Summer $88–$145 double. Lower rates in winter. AE, DISC, MC, V. **Amenities:** Large outdoor heated pool; playground; coin-op laundry. *In room:* A/C, TV.

Desert Pearl Inn 🅐   This imposing property offers luxurious and comfortable accommodations with beautiful views of the area's scenery from private terraces or balconies. Spacious rooms are decorated in modern Southwest style, with either two queens or one king bed. The grounds are nicely landscaped. Plans call for construction of a restaurant, and additional units.

707 Zion Park Blvd., Springdale, UT 84767. ✆ **888/828-0898** or 435/772-8888. Fax 435/772-8889. www.desertpearl.com. 60 units. $78–$170 double. AE, DISC, MC, V. **Amenities:** Huge outdoor heated pool; hot tub. *In room:* A/C, TV, dataport, fridge, microwave, wet bar, bidet.

Driftwood Lodge   Beautiful lawns and gardens enhance this attractive, well-kept motel—a quiet, lush complex perfect for sitting back and admiring the spectacular rock formations that practically surround the town. Extensively renovated in 1994, the spacious rooms have white walls and light wood-grain furnishings; many have patios or balconies. Most standard rooms have two queen-size beds; others have either one queen or a king. The two family suites each have one king-size and two queen beds.

1515 Zion Park Blvd. (P.O. Box 98), Springdale, UT 84767. ✆ **888/801-8811** or 435/772-3262. Fax 435/772-3702. www.driftwoodlodge.net. 47 units. Apr–Oct $72–$82 double; $102–$110 family unit. Nov–Mar $62–$72 double; $92–$100 family unit. All rates include continental breakfast. AE, DC, DISC, MC, V. Pets accepted at management's discretion. **Amenities:** Convenience store with soup and salad bar, snacks, and drinks; outdoor heated pool; whirlpool; art gallery. *In room:* A/C, TV.

El Rio Lodge in Zion Canyon 🅐 *Finds*   Our choice when we're running low on cash, the El Rio is a pleasant mom-and-pop operation with one suite, five rooms upstairs, and five downstairs, all offering private bathrooms and tub/shower combos. The motel was built in the early 1960s, and although small, the rooms are clean and comfortable, with light-colored walls and simple but attractive decor. The upstairs rooms have two double beds, with an outdoor walkway and porch affording terrific views of Zion Canyon. The downstairs rooms each have one queen bed. The suite has its own private parking area, refrigerator, microwave, extra-large bathroom, and use of a private yard, with a table and chairs and great views of the rock walls of Zion Canyon. Although there are no phones in the rooms, a public phone is available outside.

995 Zion Park Blvd. (P.O. Box 204), Springdale, UT 84767. ✆ **888/772-3205** or 435/772-3205. Fax 435/772-2455. www.elriolodge.com. 11 units. Summer $47–$52 double; $60 suite. Lower rates in winter. AE, DISC, MC, V. Pets accepted for a $10 fee. *In room:* A/C, TV, no phone.

Flanigan's Inn ★★   A mountain-lodge atmosphere pervades this very attractive complex of natural wood and rock, set among trees, lawns, and flowers just outside the entrance to Zion National Park. In fact, you might actually want to spend time here, unlike some other options in the area, which are simply good places to sleep at the end of long days spent exploring Zion. Parts of the inn date to 1947, but all rooms have been completely renovated, with Southwest decor, wood furnishings, and local art. One room has a fireplace; other units have whirlpool tubs and bidets. Flanigan's has its own nature trail leading to a hilltop vista. Summer reservations are often booked 3 to 4 months in advance.

428 Zion Park Blvd. (P.O. Box 100), Springdale, UT 84767. ℂ 800/765-7787 or 435/772-3244. Fax 435/772-3396. www.flanigans.com. 39 units. Mid-Mar to Nov $79–$99 double; Dec to mid-Mar $49–$69 double. AE, DISC, MC, V. **Amenities:** Restaurant (see "Where to Eat," later in this chapter); outdoor heated pool; spa. *In room:* A/C, TV, units with kitchenettes available.

Harvest House Bed & Breakfast at Zion   Personal touches and yummy breakfasts make this B&B a good alternative to a standard motel. This Utah territorial-style house was built in 1989 and has a cactus garden out front and a garden sitting area in back, with a koi (Japanese carp) pond and spectacular views of the park. Rooms are charming, comfortable, and quiet, with private bathrooms; they're furnished with an eclectic mixture of contemporary and wicker items, and original art and photography dot the walls. One upstairs room faces west and has grand sunset views, while the other two have private decks facing the impressive formations of Zion. The downstairs suite can accommodate up to five adults.

The gourmet breakfasts are sumptuous yet low fat, and include fresh-baked breads, fresh-squeezed orange juice, granola, fruit, yogurt, and a hot main course that changes daily.

29 Canyon View Dr. (P.O. Box 125), Springdale, UT 84767. ℂ 435/772-3880. Fax 435/772-3327. www.harvesthouse.net. 4 units. $80–$110 double. Rates include full breakfast. DISC, MC, V. Children over 6 welcome. **Amenities:** Outdoor whirlpool. *In room:* A/C, no phone.

O'Toole's Bed & Breakfast ★   Owners Rick and Michelle O'Toole have furnished this lovely 1929 home with many family antiques, creating an inn that is both attractive and comfortable. We especially enjoy the historic ambience. On the first floor there are two cheerful rooms, decorated in early-20th-century style. Each has one double bed and a private sink, and they share a bathroom (shower only). Upstairs is a 1,100-square foot suite with a vaulted ceiling, a wood-burning stove, its own kitchen, and a claw-foot tub in the bathroom. There is a queen bed and queen futon, and views of the gardens and national park. The cute Garden Cottage, which was moved here from inside the national park, contains two small but comfortable rooms, each with one queen-size bed. In the backyard is an attractive garden area with seating and a gas barbecue. Massages and facials are available by appointment for an additional fee. Breakfast generally includes home-baked breads, fresh fruit, and a hot main dish such as omelets or pancakes.

980 Zion Park Blvd. (P.O. Box 29), Springdale, UT 84767. (C) **435/772-3457** (voice/fax). www.otooles.com. 5 units (2 with shared bathroom). Apr–Oct $69–$79 double; $125 double suite. Lower rates off-season. Rates include full breakfast. DISC, MC, V. *In room:* A/C, no phone.

Snow Family Guest Ranch 🌟🌟

If you want to enjoy a stay at a horse ranch during your national park vacation, this is the place to be. Nestled in the shadow of Zion National Park on 12 acres of green pastures, all enclosed in white rail fences, this lovely horse ranch is about 12 miles west of the park and about 30 miles east of St. George. Rooms are individually decorated with an elegant western flair, with handsome log furnishings and one or two queen-size beds, a king, or two twins. The large bridal suite has a massive log bed, jetted tub and separate shower, and a TV. All rooms have private bathrooms, and most have comfortable window seats. Views from the rooms look out across the ranch to the silent red rock mesas and canyons beyond. A full breakfast is served each morning, and light refreshments are offered in the afternoon. Guests share a living room with piano, and a separate TV room with a big-screen TV. Guided scenic trail rides are offered for an additional charge.

633 E. Utah 9 (P.O. Box 790190), Virgin, UT 84779. (C) **877/655-7669** or 435/635-2500. Fax 435/635-4720. www.snowfamilyranch.com. 9 units. $89–$149 double. Rates include full breakfast. AE, DISC, MC, V. **Amenities:** Outdoor pool; hot tub; gazebo; pond. *In room:* A/C, no phone.

Terrace Brook Lodge

Reasonable rates for clean, well-maintained rooms are what you'll find here. This comfortable, older motel has Southwest decor with light wood furnishings. Four rooms have shower only; the rest have shower/tub combos. There are two barbecue and picnic areas.

990 Zion Park Blvd. (P.O. Box 217), Springdale, UT 84767. (C) **800/342-6779** or 435/772-3932. Fax 435/772-3596. www.terracebrooklodge.com. 26 units. $49–$65 double; $79–$99 suite. AE, DISC, MC, V. **Amenities:** Outdoor pool. *In room:* A/C, TV, 10 units have phones.

Zion Park Motel This economical motel, which has recently been remodeled, offers comfortable, attractively furnished rooms, with showers or shower/tub combos. A self-service laundry, a small but well-stocked grocery store with camping supplies and an ATM, and a restaurant are adjacent.

855 Zion Park Blvd. (P.O. Box 365), Springdale, UT 84767. ℭ 435/772-3251. 21 units. $59–$69 double; $79–$99 family suite. AE, DISC, MC, V. **Amenities:** Outdoor heated pool; picnic area; playground. *In room:* A/C, TV, fridge, microwave, full kitchens in 2 units.

NEAR THE EAST ENTRANCE TO ZION NATIONAL PARK

Although there is no town directly outside the east entrance to Zion National Park, there are several businesses that provide visitor services. About 13 miles east of the east entrance, at the junction of Utah 9 and U.S. 89, is Mt. Carmel Junction, at an elevation of 5,191 feet. The town is 73 miles southwest of Bryce Canyon National Park, and 17 miles northwest of Kanab.

For area information, contact the **Kane County Visitors Center,** 78 S. 100 East, Kanab, UT 84741 (ℭ **800/733-5263** or 435/644-5033; fax 435/644-5923; www.kaneutah.com).

Best Western Thunderbird Resort ⭐ A two-story motel with Southwest decor, the Thunderbird offers quiet, spacious, and comfortable rooms, with king or queen beds, wood furnishings, photos or artwork depicting area scenery, and a balcony or patio.

At the junction of Utah 9 and U.S. 89 (P.O. Box 5536), Mt. Carmel Junction, UT 84755. ℭ **888/848-6358** or 435/648-2203. Fax 435/648-2239. www.bwthunder bird.com. 61 units. May–Oct $84 double; $99 suite. Nov–Mar $49 double; $59 suite. Apr $63 double; $79 suite. Closed Christmas Day. AE, DC, DISC, MC, V. Small pets accepted with a $5 fee. **Amenities:** Restaurant (see "Where to Eat," below); large outdoor heated pool; whirlpool; 9-hole golf course ($10 for 9 holes, $18 for 18); gift shop; convenience store; coin-op laundry; gas station. *In room:* A/C, TV.

Golden Hills Motel The recently redecorated rooms at this economical, well-maintained motel are simply and comfortably furnished, and many have lovely views of the East Fork of the Virgin River. Suites and family units are large and especially attractive. There's complimentary coffee and tea in the morning and a gift shop with snacks.

At the junction of Utah 9 and U.S. 89 (P.O. Box 34), Mt. Carmel Junction, UT 84755. ℭ **800/648-2268** or 435/648-2268. Fax 435/648-2558. www.goldenhillsmotel. com. 32 units. May–Oct $43–$46 double; $72–$80 suite. Nov–Apr $28–$34 double; $49–$59 suite. AE, DISC, MC, V. Pets accepted at management's discretion. **Amenities:** Restaurant (see "Where to Eat," below); outdoor heated pool; coin-op laundry. *In room:* A/C, TV.

Mukuntuweep RV Park & Campground *(Value)* If you don't need anything more than a bed with a roof over it, this is the place to come. This attractive compound offers bargain rates for six basic but comfortable log cabins, a hogan (a traditional Navajo dwelling), and a teepee, all of which share the campground's bathhouse. Views of the surrounding rocks are grand. Across the street, under the same management, are a store, a restaurant (see "Zion Mt. Carmel Restaurant" under "Where to Eat," below), a curio shop, and a gas station.

About a quarter mile east of the east entrance to Zion National Park on Utah 9 (P.O. Box 193), Orderville, UT 84758. *©* 435/648-2154. www.xpressweb.com/zionpark. $25 double; campsites $15–$19. AE, DISC, MC, V. **Amenities:** Fishing pond; playground; game room. *In room:* No private bathrooms, no phone.

Zion Ponderosa Ranch Resort *(Finds)* Located in a quiet and picturesque area just outside the park, this lodge is a great choice for those who will be spending more than a few days in the area and want all that a full-service resort has to offer. Lodging is in comfortable but basic cabins, or you can camp. The large cabins have TVs, while smaller cabins do not, and there are no telephones (except in the largest unit) and no air-conditioning. The main reason to be here, though, is for the activities. You can go on trail rides, mountain biking, horseback riding, skeet and trap shooting, fishing, rappelling, climbing, and partake of a myriad of other activities. A summer day camp keeps the kids busy for up to 7 hours while adults tackle more ambitious activities. Services also include a shuttle. Rates are complicated and include all activities and meals; there are discounts for children. In the off-season, you can just rent the lodgings or camp without buying a complete package.

2 miles east of the Zion National Park east entrance, then 5 miles north on North Fork Rd. (P.O. Box 5547), Mt. Carmel, UT 84755. *©* **800/293-5444** or 435/648-2700. www.zionponderosa.com. 28 cabins. $65–$239 per person, all-inclusive lodging packages. $65 per person, all-inclusive camping packages. DISC, MC, V. **Amenities:** Outdoor pool; hot tub; tennis courts; sports equipment. *In room:* Few TVs, no phone.

2 Camping

Pets are accepted at all the following campgrounds but must be leashed.

INSIDE THE PARK

The two developed **national park campgrounds** in Zion Canyon are the best places to camp while visiting the park, if you can find a site. Both of the park's main campgrounds—**South** ⚘⚘ and **Watchman** ⚘⚘⚘—are located just inside the park's south entrance. They have paved roads, well-spaced sites, lots of trees, and that national park atmosphere you came here to enjoy. There are restrooms with flush toilets, and sites for those with disabilities. Although there are no RV hookups at South Campground, electric hookups are available in two loops in Watchman. **Lava Point,** a free primitive campground with six sites, is located on the Kolob Terrace. It has fire grates, tables, and vault toilets, but no water.

Reservations for Watchman Campground (© **800/365-2267**; http://reservations.nps.gov) can be made up to 20 days prior to arrival, and a reservation charge of $2.50 per site per night will be added to the regular camping fee. Some campers without reservations stay at nearby commercial campgrounds their first night in the area, then hurry into the park to South Campground the next morning, circling like vultures until a site becomes available.

There are no showers in the national park, but the commercial campgrounds listed below offer showers, for a fee, to those camping in the park.

OUTSIDE THE PARK

Just outside the east and south park entrances are commercial campgrounds with hot showers and RV hookups. Keep in mind that the park's visitor center, campgrounds, and most of its developed attractions are closer to the south entrance than to the east.

Mukuntuweep RV Park & Campground, located about a quarter mile east of the east entrance to Zion National Park on Utah 9 (P.O. Box 193), Orderville, UT 84758 (© **435/648-2154;** www.expressweb.com/zionpark), has some shade trees, grassy tent sites, a fishing pond, a playground, and a game room, plus great views of the surrounding rocks.

Zion Canyon Campground ⚘⚘ is on Zion Park Boulevard a half mile south of the park's south entrance (P.O. Box 99), Springdale, UT 84767 (© **435/772-3237;** fax 435/772-3844; www.zioncanyoncampground.com). Although quite crowded in summer, the campground is clean and well maintained, with tree-shaded sites and grassy tent areas. Some sites are along the Virgin River, and the campground also has cable TV hookups, a swimming pool, a game room, a playground, and a store.

In addition to the two commercial campgrounds discussed here, there is also camping at Cedar Breaks National Monument and Snow Canyon State Park (see chapter 9, "Nearby Things to See & Do").

Amenities for Each Campground, Zion National Park

Campground	Elev.	Total Sites	RV Hookups	Dump Station	Toilets	Drinking Water	Showers	Fire Pits/ Grills	Public Phone	Laundry	Reserve	Fees	Open
Lava Point	7,900	6	0	no	yes	no	no	yes	no	no	no	Free	May–Oct
South	4,000	126	0	yes	yes	yes	no	yes	no	yes	no	$14	Apr–Sept
Watchman	4,000	231	50+	yes	yes	yes	no	yes	no	yes	yes	$14–$16	Year-round
Mukuntuweep	6,000	150	30	yes	yes	yes	yes	yes	yes	yes	yes	$15–$19	Year-round
Zion Canyon	3,800	180	102	yes	yes	yes	yes	yes	yes	yes	yes	$16–$20	Year-round

3 Where to Eat

Those looking for picnic supplies won't find any stores inside Zion National Park, but Springdale, just outside the park's south entrance, has several. There's also a small store just outside the east entrance to the park. See the Fast Facts entry for "Supplies" in chapter 3, "Exploring Zion National Park."

INSIDE THE PARK

Zion Lodge 🐸🐸 AMERICAN   Large windows facing the park's magnificent rock formations complete the dining room's mountain lodge atmosphere. Although the menu changes periodically, it's likely to include an excellent slow-roasted prime rib au jus and the very popular Utah red mountain trout. The menu often also includes broiled salmon and several chicken dishes, such as a skinless chicken breast basted with a spicy Caribbean sauce and served with a red onion relish. There are also vegetarian items, such as pasta marissa and black bean ragout. We heartily recommend the lodge's specialty ice creams and other desserts. At lunch you'll usually find the trout, barbecued pork ribs, several dinner salads such as chicken Caesar salad and Grecian vegetarian salad, and burgers and sandwiches. The usual American selections are offered for breakfast, plus an excellent breakfast buffet. The restaurant will pack lunches to go and offers full liquor service.

Zion National Park. 📞 **435/772-3213.** www.zionlodge.com. Dinner reservations required in summer. Breakfast $4.95–$9.95; lunch $4.75–$12.95; main dinner courses $9.95–$20.25. AE, DC, DISC, MC, V. Daily 6:30–10am, 11:30am–3pm, and 5:30–9pm.

Zion Lodge's Castle Dome Cafe 🐸 SNACK BAR   Located at the north end of the lodge, this simple fast food restaurant offers an outdoor dining patio serving hot dogs, burgers, sandwiches, pizza, ice cream, frozen yogurt, and similar fare. No alcoholic beverages are served.

Zion National Park. 📞 **435/772-3213.** $3–$8. No credit cards. Daily 7am–9pm.

OUTSIDE THE PARK
SPRINGDALE & VIRGIN

Bit & Spur Restaurant & Saloon 🐸🐸 MEXICAN/SOUTHWESTERN   Rough wood-and-stone walls and an exposed beamed ceiling give this restaurant the look of an Old West saloon, but it's an unusually clean saloon that also has a family dining room, patio dining, and original oil paintings on the walls. The food here is also a notch or two above what might be expected; closer to what you'd find in a good Santa Fe restaurant. The menu includes Mexican standards such as burritos, flautas, chiles rellenos, and a traditional chile stew with pork and rice, but you'll also find more exotic creations, such as *pollo relleno*—a grilled breast of chicken stuffed with cilantro pesto and goat cheese, and served with pineapple salsa. Also good are the deep-dish chicken enchilada, with scallions, green chilies, and cheese; and the Moroccan spiced lamb—a braised lamb shank with a sweet tamarind glaze, black-eyed pea ragout, and rice. Several vegetarian items are also available. The Bit & Spur has full liquor service and an extensive wine list.

1212 Zion Park Blvd., Springdale. ℭ 435/772-3498. Reservations recommended. Main courses $7–$16.50. DISC, MC, V. Feb–Nov daily 5–10pm (bar open until midnight); weekend brunch available May–Sept (call for hours); Dec–Jan Thurs–Mon 5–10pm. Closed Christmas Day.

Panda Garden CHINESE   Chinese art, soft music, and green plants create a pleasant ambience in this large, open room. You can sit inside or on the patio. Lunch offers a wide variety of items including chow mein (chicken, pork, or beef) and sweet and sour pork or chicken. You can also get hot and spicy choices such as Hunan beef and Yu-shang shrimp. The dinner menu lists more than 50 Chinese dishes, with a dozen seafood choices plus numerous beef and chicken selections. Chef's specials include Triple Delight—gan-shiao spicy shrimp, chicken broccoli, and beef snow peas; and New York steak Chinese style—a 10-ounce steak cooked in a very hot wok with fresh vegetables, all in a rich broth. Beer is served.

805 Zion Park Blvd., Springdale. ℭ 435/772-3535. Lunch $4.95–$6.95; dinner $7.25–$18.95. AE, DISC, MC, V. Daily noon–11pm. Closed Nov–Feb.

Reese's Log House Restaurant ⭐ AMERICAN   This magnificent log structure—built with logs salvaged from the 1988 fire in Yellowstone National Park—boasts splendid views from every window. The casual atmosphere is reflected in the high-beamed ceiling, log walls, simple western decor, solid wood tables, and cushioned chairs. Slate tile from India was used on the floor. Hot sandwiches are offered for lunch, including the standard burger, plus turkey, chicken breast, fish, and steak; and cold deli sandwiches, soup, pasta, and salads. The dinner menu includes chicken fried steak, a turkey breast tenderloin steak, several beef steaks, and the Log House specialty chicken dinner. Beer and wine are available.

The huge building also houses a gift shop, a desk offering national park information, a western clothing store, and a North

American wildlife exhibit—deer, elk, Alaskan brown bear, polar bear, and a variety of fish including a great white shark.

2400 Zion Park Blvd., Springdale. ✆ 435/772-3000. Reservations not accepted. Main courses lunch $4.95–$8.95; dinner $8.95–$21.95. AE, DC, DISC, MC, V. Summer, daily 11:30am–9pm; reduced hours in winter.

Spotted Dog Café ♠ AMERICAN/REGIONAL   With a greenhouse/garden atmosphere, this restaurant makes the most of the area's spectacular scenery, with large windows for inside diners plus an outdoor patio. The chef uses fresh local ingredients and herbs from the inn's garden whenever possible. Breakfast features homemade granola, fresh fruits and juices, and various egg dishes, including trout and eggs and wonderful omelets such as smoked salmon and brie. The dinner menu changes with the seasons, with spring seeing numerous fresh vegetable and lamb dishes; summer celebrated with innovative salads and light entrees, such as local trout and mesquite roasted chicken; and fall accentuated with rich sauces, black Angus beef, pork, wild game, and scrumptious desserts. Vegan dishes can be individually prepared. There is a 2,000-bottle wine cellar; microbrewery draft beers are available as well.

At Flanigan's Inn, 428 Zion Park Blvd., Springdale. ✆ 435/772-3244. Reservations recommended. Main courses $8.95–$18. AE, DISC, MC, V. Daily 7am–11:30am and 5–10pm; reduced hours in winter.

Zion Park Gift & Deli ♠ *Value* SANDWICHES   This is our choice for a top quality deli-style sandwich at an economical price. You can eat at one of the cafe-style tables inside, on the outdoor patio, or carry your sandwich off on a hike or to a national park picnic ground. All baked goods, including the excellent sandwich breads and sub rolls, are made in-house. In typical deli style, you order at the counter and wait as your meal is prepared with your choice of bread, meats, cheeses, and condiments. This is also a good breakfast stop for those who enjoy fresh-baked cinnamon rolls, muffins, banana nut bread, and similar goodies, with a cup of espresso. Locally made candy and 16 flavors of ice cream and frozen yogurt are also offered. No alcohol is served.

866 Zion Park Blvd., Springdale. ✆ 435/772-3843. $5–$10. AE, DISC, MC, V. Summer, Mon–Sat 8am–9pm; reduced hours in winter.

Zion Pizza & Noodle ♠ *Kids* PIZZA/PASTA   This busy cafe is the place to come for good pizza and pasta in a somewhat funky atmosphere—it's located in a former church with a turquoise steeple. The dining room has small, closely spaced tables and black-and-white photos on the walls. Patrons order at the counter and help themselves to soft drinks while waiting for their food to be delivered. The 12-inch pizzas, with lots of chewy crust, are baked in a slate stone oven. They're very good, but we were initially put off by all the oddly-topped specialty pies, such as the Southwest burrito pizza or barbecue chicken pizza. But have no fear—you can get a basic cheese pizza or add any of the roughly 15 extra toppings, from pepperoni to green chilies to pineapple. The menu also offers a variety of pastas, such as penne pasta with grilled chicken, broccoli, carrots, fresh cream, and cheese; calzones; and stromboli. Take out and delivery service are provided. Beer is available.

868 Zion Park Blvd., Springdale. ✆ 435/772-3815. www.zionpizzanoodle.com. Reservations not accepted. Entrees $7.95–$11.95. No credit cards. Daily from 4pm; call for winter hours.

OUTSIDE THE EAST ENTRANCE TO ZION NATIONAL PARK

Golden Hills Restaurant AMERICAN   This is a simply but attractively decorated family-style restaurant, where you'll find made-from-scratch breads, pies, and soups. We especially like the casual, homey atmosphere here. Breakfasts include the usual egg and pancake offerings; lunch is burgers and sandwiches, a soup and salad bar, plus scones with butter and honey. For dinner you can get steak, chicken, fish, pork, and pasta. We especially recommend the country-fried steak and cream of broccoli soup. Beer and wine are served.

At the junction of Utah 9 and U.S. 89 at the Golden Hills Motel. ✆ 435/648-2602. Reservations not accepted. Lunch $3.25–$5.25; dinner $7.95–$16.95. MC, V. Summer daily 7am–10pm; winter daily 8am–8pm.

Thunderbird Restaurant AMERICAN   This spacious restaurant offers both booths and tables in a comfortable, Southwest setting. The decor is simple and attractive, in pastels with wood accents. The breakfast menu includes pancakes, French toast, cereal, fruit, breads, numerous egg dishes, and even a hearty steak and eggs platter. Lunch consists of a wide variety of sandwiches and burgers. Dinner entrees include steak, seafood, and chicken, plus the popular country-fried steak. The restaurant has great homemade pies, breads, and soups, and a soup and salad bar is open at dinner during the summer. Beer and wine are served.

At the junction of Utah 9 and U.S. 89 in the Best Western Thunderbird Resort. ✆ 435/648-2203. Reservations not accepted. Lunch $4.95–$7.95; dinner entrees $8.95–$17.95. AE, DC, DISC, MC, V. Summer daily 7am–10pm; winter daily 7am–8pm. Closed Christmas Day.

Zion Mt. Carmel Restaurant AMERICAN/MEXICAN This down-home coffee shop offers great homemade pies, spicy New Mexico–style Southwest dishes, shakes and sundaes, and burgers and sandwiches. Locals love the green chile beef and bean burrito, and the enchilada-style burrito, which is smothered with chile sauce. The breakfast menu includes the standards: ham and eggs, omelets, pancakes, and French toast. No alcoholic beverages are served.

A quarter mile east of the east entrance to Zion National Park (P.O. Box 193, Orderville, UT 84758). (C) **435/648-2829.** Breakfast $3.25–$5.95; sandwiches $3.50–$5.50; Mexican dishes $2.95–$7.95. AE, DISC, MC, V. Daily 9am–5pm.

6

Exploring Bryce Canyon National Park

The scenic beauty of Bryce Canyon National Park is unsurpassed—and because it is among the West's most accessible parks, its wonders can be enjoyed by everyone from the very young to the very old, and from hearty backpackers to visitors in wheelchairs. Bryce's defining feature is its hoodoos—those rock formations that delight the child in all of us. But look a bit deeper and you'll discover Bryce Canyon's other faces, from its varied wildlife to its rugged forests.

1 Essentials

GETTING THERE/GATEWAYS Situated in the mountains of southern Utah, the park is crossed east-west by Utah 12. The bulk of the park, including the visitor center, is accessed by Utah 63, which turns south off Utah 12 into the main portions of the park. U.S. 89 runs north-south west of the park, and Utah 12 heads east to Tropic and eventually to Escalante.

VISITOR CENTER & INFORMATION The visitor center, at the north end, just after you enter the park, has exhibits on the geology and history of the area and presents an excellent introductory video program on the park, which we recommend seeing if you have time. There are large photos of many of the park's better-known formations, and a relief map that shows Bryce Canyon and nearby sections of the Colorado Plateau, including Grand Staircase–Escalante National Monument. Rangers can answer questions and provide backcountry permits; several free brochures are available; and books, maps, videos, postcards, and posters are sold. The visitor center is open daily year-round except Thanksgiving, Christmas, and New Year's days. Summer hours are usually from 8am to 8pm, with shorter hours the rest of the year.

FEES   Entry into the park (for up to 7 days) costs $20 per private vehicle, which includes unlimited use of the park shuttle (when it's operating). Cost is $15 for those who leave their vehicles outside the park and ride the shuttle. A $30 annual pass is also available. Campsites cost $10 per night.

Backcountry permits, which cost $5 and are available at the visitor center daily until 8pm, are required for all overnight trips into the backcountry, and backcountry camping is permitted on only two trails, with details at the visitor center.

REGULATIONS & WARNINGS   Backcountry hikers should practice minimum-impact techniques; they are prohibited from building fires and must carry their own water, as water sources in the backcountry are considered unreliable. Bicycles are prohibited in the backcountry and on all trails. Feeding or molesting wildlife, vandalism, and disturbing any natural feature of the park are all prohibited. Pets, which must be leashed at all times, are prohibited on all trails, in the backcountry, and in public buildings.

Trailers are not permitted beyond Sunset Campground; they can be left in a campsite, at the visitor center, or in other designated parking areas. Any vehicle longer than 25 feet (large trucks and motor homes, for instance) cannot go to Paria View.

While most visitors to Bryce Canyon enjoy an exciting vacation without mishap, accidents can occur, and here—possibly because of the nature of the trails—the most common injuries by far are sprained, twisted, and broken ankles. Park rangers strongly recommend that hikers—even those out on short day hikes—wear sturdy hiking boots with good traction and ankle support.

A concern in the park in recent years has been **bubonic plague,** which, contrary to popular belief, is treatable with antibiotics if caught early. The bacteria that causes bubonic plague has been found on fleas in prairie dog colonies in the park, so you should avoid contact with wild animals, especially prairie dogs and other rodents. Those taking pets into the park should dust them with flea powder. Avoiding contact with infected animals will greatly minimize the chances of contracting the plague, but caution is still necessary.

Symptoms, which generally occur from 2 to 6 days after exposure, may include high fever, headache, vomiting, diarrhea, and swollen glands. Anyone with these symptoms following a park visit should get medical attention immediately, because the plague can be fatal if not treated promptly.

FAST FACTS: Bryce Canyon National Park

ATMs Just outside the entrance to the park, there is an automated teller machine (ATM) in the lobby of Ruby's Inn (✆ 435/834-5341).

Car Trouble/Towing Services Located just outside the entrance to the park, **Bryce Canyon American Car Care Center** (✆ 435/834-5232) is a full-service station, with facilities to work on large vehicles and motor homes, and offers AAA towing service (✆ 435/834-5222), a car wash, and car rentals.

Emergencies Dial ✆ 911, call the Garfield County Sheriff's office (✆ 435/676-2411), or contact a park ranger.

Gas Stations Just outside the entrance to the park are two gas stations (Chevron and Texaco) operated by Ruby's Inn. There are also gas stations along Utah 12 in Bryce and Tropic.

Laundry Inside the park there is a coin-operated laundry at the General Store, about a quarter mile south of North Campground near the Sunrise Point parking area. It's open daily from mid-April to October.

Just outside the entrance to the park, Ruby's Inn has two coin-operated laundries. The one in the main complex is open 24 hours a day year-round, and the second, located at Ruby's Campground about a quarter mile south of the inn, is open April through October from 7am to 9:30pm daily.

Medical Services There is a first-aid station at Bryce Canyon Lodge. The closest hospital is the **Garfield Memorial Hospital and Clinic,** 224 N. 400 E. in Panguitch, 24 miles northwest via Utah 12 and U.S. 89 (✆ 435/676-8811), which has a 24-hour emergency room.

Permits Permits are required for backcountry camping. They cost $5 and are available at the visitor center until 8pm daily.

Post Offices Inside the main building of Ruby's Inn is the Bryce Post Office (ZIP 84764). The Bryce Canyon Lodge also has a post office (Bryce Canyon, ZIP 84717), open April through October.

Supplies There is a small general store (contact **Bryce Lodge,** ✆ 435/834-5361) inside the park that is open from mid-April to October, with groceries and camping supplies, plus snacks, film, ice, beer, bundles of firewood, and souvenirs, all at surprisingly reasonable prices. Hours are from 8am to 8pm daily, although these are flexible and the store is sometimes open a bit longer in summer, with shorter hours at the beginning and end of the season.

On the south side of the lobby of **Ruby's Inn** (② 435/834-5341), just outside the entrance to the park, is a huge general store that offers souvenirs, western clothing, camping supplies, and a good selection of groceries. The store is open from 7am to 10:30pm daily. In the lobby is a small liquor store, a car-rental desk, a beauty salon, a 1 hour film processor, and tour desks where you can arrange excursions of all sorts, from horseback and all-terrain-vehicle rides to helicopter tours.

Telephones Public telephones are located at the visitor center, Bryce Canyon Lodge, Sunset Campground pay station, and the General Store. There is also a public phone at Ruby's Inn, just north of the park entrance.

Weather Updates For current statewide weather information, contact the **National Weather Service** (② 801/524-5133; http://nimbo.wrh.noaa.gov/saltlake). For local weather information, call the park office (② 435/834-5322).

2 Tips from a Park Ranger

Former park ranger Dave Mecham says it's easy to pinpoint Bryce Canyon's most striking feature—it's the hoodoos.

"They're photogenic, stunningly beautiful. You can find free-standing rock formations throughout the world, but I don't think there's any place where hoodoos are this numerous, this delicately eroded, or beautifully colored." (For a discussion of the geologic forces that form hoodoos, see chapter 10, "A Nature Guide to Zion & Bryce Canyon National Parks.")

But what Mecham enjoys most about the park is not necessarily its most recognizable feature. He prefers standing on the rim and simply relishing the views: "Looking out from the rim of Bryce, across the hoodoos, it seems you can see forever. The atmospheric conditions are almost ideal, and you get the feeling that you're looking at a piece of America that's still pretty wild, and just hasn't changed much through time."

Bryce Amphitheater ⚑⚑⚑ has the best scenery in the park, in Mecham's opinion: "It's the place in the park where everything's coming together geologically to carve hoodoos at their best."

Bryce Canyon National Park

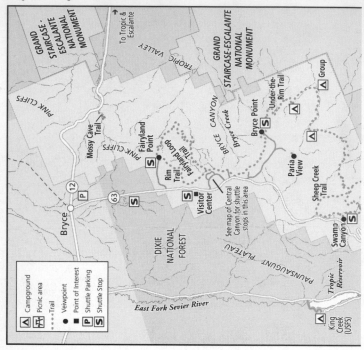

Mecham particularly enjoys the **Rim Trail** that runs along the edge of the canyon and highly recommends the section between Inspiration and Bryce Points, with perhaps the very best view from a section known as **Upper Inspiration Point,** which is 300 to 400 yards south of Inspiration Point.

Among Mecham's favorite trails is the **Fairyland Loop** ✿✿, which takes about 4 hours. To get the best views, start at Sunrise Point, go down past Tower Bridge, and back up through Fairyland Canyon to Fairyland Trail Head. Then take the Rim Trail back to Sunrise Point. "It's 5 miles below the rim and then 3 miles of Rim Trail. Fairyland Canyon is beautiful—the highlight of that loop—and as you come around the bend, you're hiking straight toward a really beautiful backdrop. If you're going the opposite direction, you have to keep stopping to look over your shoulder."

Mecham calls Bryce Canyon a "morning park," because, with only a few exceptions, the views are much better illuminated by early morning light than at any other time of day. To get the most

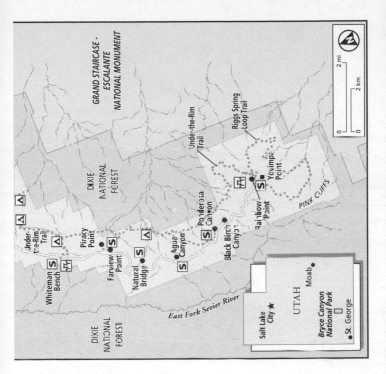

out of your visit, he recommends spending at least 1 night at or near the park: "If you're spending the night close by, I think it would be a big mistake to miss sunrise—in the middle of the summer that's getting up before 6."

Getting up early is also the best way to avoid crowds, according to Mecham, since most people don't get to the viewpoints or onto the trails until about 10am. The other way to avoid crowds is to walk away from them. Mecham says that you're likely not to see anyone at all on the park's two backcountry trails at the south end of the park; but avoiding crowds, even in the park's most popular areas, often takes only a short walk. "**Sunset Point** is probably the busiest place in the park, especially in midsummer at midday," he says. "You finally get a parking spot, then walk out to a very crowded viewpoint, where you're standing shoulder to shoulder— it's real hectic—but if you take a 5-minute walk south along the Rim Trail toward Inspiration Point, you'll leave the people immediately—they just cluster at those views."

Wildlife Viewing

Bryce Canyon has a wide variety of wildlife, ranging from mule deer—which seem to be almost everywhere—to the golden-mantled ground squirrel and Uinta chipmunk. Also in the park are black-tailed jackrabbits, coyotes, striped skunks, and deer mice. Occasionally visitors catch a glimpse of a mountain lion, most likely on the prowl in search of a mule-deer dinner. Elk and pronghorn may also be seen at higher elevations.

The Utah prairie dog, listed as a threatened species, is actually a rodent and not a distant canine relative. It inhabits park meadows in busy colonies and can be fascinating to watch. However, don't get too close because its fleas may carry disease (see "Regulations & Warnings," above).

Of the many birds in the park, you're bound to hear the obnoxious call of the Steller's jay. Other birds often seen include violet-green swallows, common ravens, Clark's nutcrackers, American robins, red-shafted flickers, dark-eyed juncos, and chipping sparrows. Watch for white-throated swifts as they perform their exotic acrobatics along cliff faces. The park is also home, at least part of the year, to peregrine falcons, red-tailed hawks, golden eagles, bald eagles, and great horned owls.

The Great Basin rattlesnake, although pretty, should be given a wide berth. Sometimes growing to more than 5 feet long, this rattler is the park's only poisonous reptile. Happily, like most rattlesnakes, it is just as anxious as you are to avoid a confrontation. Other reptiles you may see are the mountain short-horned lizard, tree lizard, side-blotched lizard, and northern sagebrush lizard.

For detailed information on many of these animals, plus the various plants you'll encounter in the park, see chapter 10, "A Nature Guide to Zion & Bryce Canyon National Parks."

Mecham says that September and October are probably the best times to visit the park. "It's still busy," he says, "but less crowded on trails." However, if you really want to avoid people, you'll feel you have the park all to yourself if you visit midweek in the middle of

the winter. "We plow the roads so people can drive to the viewpoints and photograph the canyon with snow on it, and the people
that ski or snowshoe will enjoy it the most." He adds, "Skiing is at
its best in January and February, when it's really cold."

3 The Highlights

Everyone should spend at least a little time on the park's **scenic
drive,** following the canyon rim south to Rainbow Point. There are
numerous stops where you can get off the shuttle or out of your
vehicle and gaze into the canyon to view the varicolored formations
and trail heads that provide access down into the amphitheaters.
(For more information on this and other drives, see "Seeing the Park
by Car," below; also check out chapter 7, "Hikes & Other Outdoor
Pursuits in Bryce Canyon National Park," where you'll find detailed
information on all the hiking trails and activities mentioned in this
section).

Another top experience is walking the **Rim Trail** for at least a
short way, to access different views into Bryce Amphitheater.
Although it's worthwhile at any time of day, the Rim Trail is especially wonderful just after sunrise, in time to catch the changing
angles of the sun on the hoodoos.

One viewpoint not to be missed is the appropriately named
Inspiration Point *★★★*, which provides a splendid view down
into Bryce Amphitheater, the park's largest and most colorful natural amphitheater. It provides the best view of **Silent City,** which is
packed with hoodoos and leads the imagination to unexpected
heights. Some of us, however, believe the view is even better—possibly the best in the park—just south of Inspiration Point along the
Rim Trail, up a little rise, at what is usually called **Upper
Inspiration Point** *★★★*.

To really get a feel for the canyon and grand close-up views of
many spectacular formations, you must hike down into it to walk
among the hoodoos. Among the various trails from which to
choose, one of the best is the **Queen's Garden Trail** *★★★*, which

---

Tips **A Tip for Picnickers**

On a hot summer day, the best spot in the park for a picnic
lunch is Rainbow Point, where you'll find picnic tables and
restrooms. It's also among the coolest areas because, at 9,115
feet elevation, it's the highest point in the park.

Tips   Restrooms at Bryce Canyon

The nicest and most modern restrooms at Bryce Canyon are at the visitor center and just off the lobby at Bryce Lodge. They're well maintained, heated, and have flush toilets and sinks with hot water.

There are also restrooms with hot water at the General Store in the park, and just outside the park entrance at Ruby's Inn (just off the lobby).

Other park facilities range from flush toilets at North and Sunset Campgrounds and Sunset Point to vault toilets at Rainbow, Yovimpa, and Farview points. Although there are few toilets along trails (none in the backcountry), spring through fall you will find a vault toilet on the Peekaboo Loop Trail, just west of its intersection with the Bryce Point cutoff trail.

Although essentially outhouses, vault toilets—officially called "bulk-reduction toilet systems"—have come a long way in the past 20 years—they're now clean, sanitary, and best of all they don't smell. However, there is no water for hand washing, no lights, and no heat. During busy times, the less-developed restroom facilities may run out of toilet paper, so it's best to carry a backup supply.

can be completed in only a few hours, is easy enough for most park visitors—including children—and takes you to some fascinating hoodoos.

Speaking of hoodoos, there are a few that are on almost everyone's must-see list. These naturally sculpted monuments in stone include majestic Queen Victoria, which can be seen from Sunrise Point on the rim, but is better examined from the Queen's Garden Trail. Another is magnificent Thor's Hammer, which is visible from Sunset Point but best seen from the Navajo Loop Trail.

Attractions that aren't made of stone include Bryce Canyon's **bristlecone pine trees,** exceptionally old evergreens that grow in some of the more inhospitable areas of the park. They're easily seen via the Bristlecone Loop Trail. See chapter 10, "A Nature Guide to Zion & Bryce Canyon National Parks."

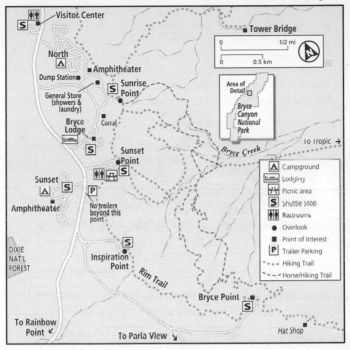

4 How to See the Park in 1 or 2 Days

It would be easy to spend a week in Bryce Canyon, starting with the visitor center, then moving along to the scenic drive, a few short walks, and then advancing to more serious hikes. But what makes this park so attractive to many of us is that there are ways to see a good deal of Bryce in a short amount of time.

Get an early start, stopping first at the **visitor center,** of course, where you can watch the introductory video that explains some of the area's geology—the *why* and *how* of Bryce. Then either drive the 18-mile (each way) dead-end **park road,** stopping at viewpoints to gaze down into the canyon (see "Seeing the Park by Car," below), or hop on the **Bryce Canyon Scenic Tours & Shuttles** van for a 1½- to 2-hour guided tour, complete with lively commentary (see "Guided Tours," below). An alternative is to take the new **shuttle system** (discussed below), which will take you to most of the main viewpoints. Whichever way you choose to get around, spend at least a little time at **Inspiration Point,** which offers a splendid (and yes, inspirational) view into **Bryce Amphitheater** and its hundreds of statuesque pink, red, orange, and brown hoodoo stone sculptures.

After seeing the canyon from the top down, we recommend you get some exercise by walking at least part way down the **Queen's Garden Trail.** If you can spare 3 hours, hike down the **Navajo Loop Trail** and return to the rim via **Queen's Garden Trail** (both are described in the chapter 7, "Hikes & Other Outdoor Pursuits in Bryce Canyon National Park"). Those not willing or physically able to hike into the canyon can enjoy a leisurely walk along the **Rim Trail,** which provides spectacular views down into the canyon. In the evening, try to take in the campground amphitheater program.

5 Seeing the Park by Car

The park's 18-mile (one-way) **scenic drive** ★★★ follows the rim of Bryce Canyon, offering easy access to a variety of views into the fanciful fairyland of stone sculptures below. Trailers are not permitted on the road but can be left at several parking lots. Also, because all overlooks are on your left as you begin your drive, it's best to avoid crossing traffic by driving all the way to the end of the road and stopping at the overlooks on your return. Allow 1 to 2 hours for the main viewpoints; 3 to 4 hours if you plan to do a bit of walking.

After leaving the visitor center, drive 18 miles to **Yovimpa** and **Rainbow Point** overlooks, which offer expansive views of southern Utah, Arizona, and sometimes even New Mexico. From these pink cliffs, you can look down on a colorful platoon of stone soldiers, standing at eternal attention. The short **Bristlecone Loop Trail** (described in chapter 7, "Hikes & Other Outdoor Pursuits in Bryce Canyon National Park"), from Rainbow Point, leads to an **1,800-year-old bristlecone pine,** believed to be one of the oldest living things at Bryce Canyon. Heading north, the **Black Birch Canyon Overlook** is a roadside pullout where you get a good view of the southern part of the park, including Rainbow Point.

From here, drive back north to **Ponderosa Canyon Overlook,** where you can gaze down from a dense forest of spruce and fir at multicolored hoodoos, before continuing to **Agua Canyon Overlook,** with some of the best color contrasts you'll find in the park. Look almost straight down to see **the Hunter,** a hoodoo with a hat of evergreens.

Now continue on to **Natural Bridge,** actually an arch carved by rain and wind, which spans 85 feet. From here, continue to **Farview**

Tips **The Time to Drive**

The scenic drive is practically deserted in early mornings—any time before 9am—which is also the best time to see deer, and when the light on the hoodoos is the richest.

Point, where there's a panoramic view to the distant horizon and the Kaibab Plateau at the Grand Canyon's north rim. From Farview Point, a dirt path leads several hundred yards north to **Piracy Point,** which offers good views to the north. After passing the **Swamp Canyon** overlook, continue until you see a right turn off the main road, where you'll find three viewpoints.

The first of these is **Paria View,** with views to the south of the White Cliffs, which have been carved into light-colored sandstone by the Paria River.

To the north of Paria View, you'll find **Bryce Point,** a splendid stop for seeing the awesome **Bryce Amphitheater,** the largest natural amphitheater in the park, as well as distant views of the Black Mountains to the northeast and Navajo Mountain to the south.

From here it's just a short drive back toward the main road and **Inspiration Point,** a must-see offering views similar to those at Bryce Point plus the best view in the park of the **Silent City,** a sleeping city cast in stone.

Now return to the main road and head north to **Sunset Point,** where you can see practically all of Bryce Amphitheater, including the aptly named **Thor's Hammer** and the 200-foot-tall cliffs of **Wall Street.**

Continue north to a turnoff for your final stop at **Sunrise Point,** where there's an inspiring view into Bryce Amphitheater. This is the beginning of the **Queen's Garden Trail,** an excellent choice for even a quick walk below the canyon's rim (described in chapter 7).

6 Seeing the Park by Shuttle

In recent years, congestion has been increasing along the park's only road, making a drive through the park a less than pleasurable experience. To alleviate this, a **shuttle service** is now in effect from mid-to-late May to September, between 7am and dark. Visitors can park their cars at the parking and boarding area at the intersection of the entrance road and Utah 12, 3 miles from the park boundary, and ride the shuttle. Those staying in the park at Bryce Canyon Lodge or one of the campgrounds can also use the shuttle, at no additional charge (see "Fees," earlier in this chapter).

The shuttle system is divided into three parts: the **Blue Line,** which travels between the boarding area and the visitor center about every 15 minutes, with stops at Ruby's Inn and Fairyland Point; the **Red Line,** which departs from the visitor center approximately every 15 minutes and traverses the more developed areas of the park, making eight stops daily; and the **Green Line,** which departs the visitor center several times daily for a 2½-hour drive to Rainbow Point in the southern part of the park, stopping at viewpoints on the return trip. Reservations, available at the visitor center up to 24 hours in advance, are required for the Green Line buses. Backcountry hikers are welcome to use the Green Line to access their chosen trail head, and should inform the driver they will not be returning to the bus. Check at the visitor center for the current schedule.

7 Historic & Man-Made Attractions

Although prehistoric American Indians and 19th-century pioneers spent some time in what is now Bryce Canyon National Park, they left little evidence. The park's main historic site is the handsome sandstone and ponderosa pine **Bryce Canyon Lodge** ⟨★★★⟩, built by the Union Pacific Railroad and opened in 1924. Much of it has been faithfully restored to its 1920s appearance, and the lobby contains historic photos taken in the park during that period.

8 Ranger Programs

Park rangers present a variety of free programs and activities. **Evening programs,** which may include a slide show, take place most evenings at campground amphitheaters. Topics vary, but could include such subjects as the animals and plants of the park, geology, and the role of humans in the park's early days. Rangers also give half-hour talks several times daily at various locations in the park, and lead hikes and walks, including a **moonlight hike** ⟨★★⟩ (reservations required) and a wheelchair-accessible, 1-hour **canyon rim walk** ⟨★★⟩. Schedules are posted on bulletin boards at the visitor center, general store, campgrounds, and Bryce Canyon Lodge.

Several times a week spring through fall, usually in the evening, a talk is given on the patio or in the auditorium at **Bryce Canyon Lodge.** The free talks often include some lodge history, geology of the area, and discussion of some of the park's trails. Check at the lodge or visitor center for the current schedule.

Tips **Wildlife Alert**

For a good chance to see peregrine falcons, go to Paria View, sit quietly away from the crowds, and then look out over the amphitheater, where peregrine falcons can often be spotted.

---

9 Guided Tours

Bryce Canyon Scenic Tours (© **800/432-5383** or 435/834-5200; www.brycetours.com) offers 1½- to 2-hour tours year-round, leaving from Ruby's Inn just outside the park entrance. A general tour, stopping at several viewpoints, costs $26 for adults, $12 for children 5 to 15, and is free for children under 5. Sunrise/sunset and other specialized tours are also available.

For a bird's-eye view of the canyon and its numerous formations, contact **Bryce Canyon Helicopter Scenic Flights** (ask for the flight desk at Ruby's Inn, © **435/834-5341**). Tours last from less than 20 minutes to more than an hour, and the longer trips include surrounding attractions. Prices start at $55 per person, with discounts for families and groups.

Several national **adventure tour operators** offer guided biking, hiking, and backpacking trips in and near the park, and other companies offer more traditional tour packages. See "Adventure Vacations & Organized Tours" in chapter 2.

10 Especially for Kids

Bryce Canyon is a fantasyland that kids love—even teenagers trying their hardest to be bored will have a great deal of trouble not being fascinated by the bizarre and whimsical shapes that in many ways are the essence of this park. Among the best trails for kids are **Queen's Garden** and **Navajo Loop,** which are not only fairly easy, but lead to some of the park's best hoodoos. Teenagers with a bit more stamina will probably enjoy the 8-mile **Fairyland Loop.** Details are available in the "Day Hikes" section of chapter 7.

During the summer, children 12 and younger can join the **Junior Rangers,** participate in a variety of programs, and earn certificates and patches ($1). Junior Ranger booklets are available at the visitor center. In addition, park rangers periodically conduct **special kids' activities**—usually lasting about an hour and a half—on subjects such as the park ecology. Reservations are required—contact the visitor center for information.

7

Hikes & Other Outdoor Pursuits in Bryce Canyon National Park

One of the wonderful things about Bryce Canyon is that even though hiking is the best way to explore it, you don't have to be an advanced backpacker to really get to know the park. There are ample opportunities to experience much of the park on easy walks, and many people see the park from the back of a mule or horse. In the winter, the park's trails open to snowshoers and cross-country skiers.

Several national adventure tour operators offer guided hiking and backpacking trips in and near the park; see "Adventure Vacations & Organized Tours," in chapter 2.

1 Day Hikes

Remember that all trails below the rim have at least some steep grades, so you should wear hiking boots with a traction tread and good ankle support to avoid ankle injuries, the most common accidents in the park. During the hot summer months, you'll want to hike either early or late in the day. Not only is it cooler then, but there are fewer people on the trails and the lighting on the hoodoos can produce dramatic effects. Bryce's rangers have recently stopped rating hiking trails as to their difficulty, saying that what is easy for one person may be difficult for another. Ratings here are provided by the authors and other experienced hikers, and are entirely subjective.

SHORTER HIKES

Bristlecone Loop Trail ✦✦✦ *Kids*   An easy walk entirely above the canyon rim, this trail winds among white fir, Douglas fir, and ponderosa and bristlecone pines; you'll see more bristlecones here than on any other park trail. More than many other species, the bristlecone can withstand the strong winds and harsh conditions often found on high ridges, as well as times of prolonged drought; consequently, they often live to a great age—one in California is

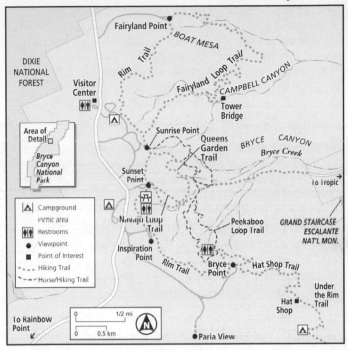

more than 4,000 years old! The oldest bristlecone pines in Bryce Canyon have been around nearly 2,000 years. The trail has an elevation change of 100 feet, and the round-trip takes about 1 hour.

1 mile RT. Easy. Access: The trail head is located at the Rainbow Point parking area at the end of the scenic drive.

Hat Shop Trail This is a strenuous hike with a 900-foot elevation change; it's also the beginning of the **Under the Rim Trail** (see "Exploring the Backcountry," later in this chapter). Leaving the rim, you'll drop quickly to the Hat Shop, so-named because it consists of a series of formations that resemble hard, gray hats perched on narrow, reddish-brown pedestals. The trail offers close-up views of gnarled ponderosa pine and Douglas fir, as well as distant panoramas across the Aquarius Plateau toward the Grand Staircase–Escalante National Monument (see chapter 9, "Nearby Things to See & Do"). This hike will take you approximately 4 hours if you go the whole distance.

4.6 miles RT. Difficult. Access: The trail head is located at the Bryce Point Overlook.

Mossy Cave Trail *Finds*   An often-overlooked trail located outside the main part of the park, the Mossy Cave Trail offers an easy and picturesque walk. The trail follows an old irrigation ditch up a short hill to a shallow cave, where seeping water nurtures the cave's namesake moss. Just off the trail, you'll also see a small waterfall. Elevation gain is 150 feet. Allow about 45 minutes for the whole trip.

0.8 miles RT. Easy. Access: The trail head is located along Utah 12, about 3½ miles east of the park access road, Utah 63.

Navajo Loop Trail 𝕲𝕲𝕲   This trail descends from the canyon rim 521 feet to the bottom of the canyon floor and back up again. Traversing graveled switchbacks, it affords terrific views of several impressive formations, including the towering skyscrapers of Wall Street, the awesome Twin Bridges, and the precariously balanced Thor's Hammer. The round-trip on this trail takes 1 to 2 hours.

1.4 miles RT. Moderate. Access: The trail head is signposted at the central overlook at Sunset Point.

Queen's Garden Trail 𝕲𝕲𝕲   This short trail, which drops 320 feet below the rim, takes you down into Bryce Amphitheater, with rest benches near the formation called **Queen Victoria.** At the beginning of the descent, keep an eye cocked to the distant views so you won't miss Boat Mesa, the Sinking Ship, the Aquarius Plateau, and Bristlecone Point. As you plunge deeper into the canyon, the trail passes some of the park's most fanciful formations, including majestic Queen Victoria herself, for whom the trail and this grouping of hoodoos are named, plus the Queen's Castle and Gulliver's Castle. The round-trip takes 1 to 2 hours.

1.8 miles RT. Moderate. Access: The trail head is located on the south side of Sunrise Point.

Tips **The Best of Two Great Trails**

A great choice for getting down into the canyon and seeing the most with the least amount of sweat is to combine **Navajo Loop Trail** with the **Queen's Garden Trail.** The total distance is just under 3 miles, and most hikers take from 2 to 3 hours. It's best to start at the Navajo Loop Trail Head at Sunset Point and leave the canyon on the less steep Queen's Garden Trail, returning to the rim at Sunrise Point, a half mile north of the Navajo Loop Trail Head.

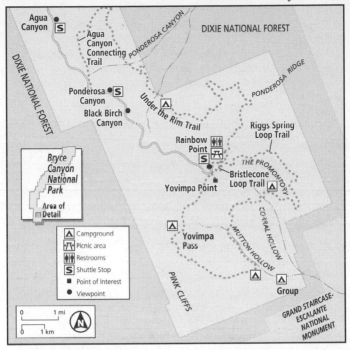

Agua
Canyon 🅂

Agua
Canyon
Connecting
Trail

PONDEROSA CANYON

DIXIE NATIONAL FOREST

DIXIE NATIONAL FOREST

PONDEROSA RIDGE

Ponderosa 🅂
Canyon

Black Birch
Canyon

Under the Rim Trail

Bryce
Canyon
National
Park

Area of
Detail

Riggs Spring
Loop Trail

Rainbow 🚻
Point 🛆

🅂

THE PROMONTORY

Bristlecone
Loop Trail

Yovimpa Point

🛆 Campground
🛆 Picnic area
🚻 Restrooms
🅂 Shuttle Stop
◼ Point of Interest
● Viewpoint

Yovimpa
Pass

MUTTON HOLLOW

CORRAL HOLLOW

PINK CLIFFS

Group

GRAND STAIRCASE-
ESCALANTE
NATIONAL
MONUMENT

0   1 mi
0   1 km

Ⓝ

LONGER HIKES

Fairyland Loop Trail ⋒⋒   From Fairyland Point, this strenuous
but little-traveled trail descends into Fairyland Canyon, then meanders up, down, and around Boat Mesa, crosses Campbell Canyon,
passes Tower Bridge junction—a short, 200-yard side trail takes you
to the base of Tower Bridge—and begins a steady climb to the
Chinese Wall. About halfway along the wall, the trail begins the serious ascent back to the top of the canyon, which it reaches near
Sunrise Point. To complete the loop, follow the Rim Trail back
through juniper, manzanita, and Douglas fir to Fairyland Point, a
trip that will take you approximately 5 hours. The loop has an elevation change of about 900 feet.

8 miles RT. Difficult. Access: The trail head is located at the Fairyland Point Overlook,
off the park access road north of the visitor center; the trail is also accessible from
Sunrise Point.

⟲ Hoodoo Photography: The "Light" Stuff

The delightful rock formations that decorate the amphitheaters at Bryce Canyon National Park beg to be photographed, and they have been—many times and from every conceivable angle. Look at those expensive, glossy calendars or the various coffee table books filled with dramatic photos of the American West. You'll see Bryce Canyon's hoodoos standing tall in almost every single one of them, with their vibrant reds and oranges set against a pure blue sky and accented by the rich greens of junipers and piñons.

This scenery is why you came, and among the best souvenirs you can take home are good quality photos that you've taken yourself. While at Bryce Canyon, you're apt to see photographers loaded down with expensive equipment, with all manner of lenses and filters; and although these tools can be helpful (and fun), the most important element of photography is not the equipment, but the photographer. The way to get good photos of Bryce Canyon's hoodoos with practically any type of camera is simple: Choose your timing for the best lighting—usually sunrise—compose carefully, and keep your camera steady.

Professional photographers are always carrying on about getting the right light, and at Bryce Canyon this is especially important. That's because of the nature of the hoodoos. In

Peekaboo Loop Trail This trail, open to both those on foot and on horseback, winds among hoodoos below Bryce and Inspiration points. It's a fairly strenuous hike, with an elevation change of 800 feet. You follow the Under the Rim Trail briefly toward the Hat Shop, but soon you'll turn left and head toward the Peekaboo Loop. This section of the trail is narrow and often littered with rocks, so place your feet carefully. Fairly steep inclines and descents alternate with more level stretches; stop frequently to take in both the close and distant vistas. At times you can see far to the east beyond Bryce Canyon toward the Aquarius Plateau, Canaan Mountain, and the Kaiparowits Plateau; you'll get closer views of the unusual Wall of Windows, the Three Wisemen, the Organ, and the Cathedral. Various connecting trails make Peekaboo easily accessible. There's a early morning (and to a somewhat lesser degree in late afternoon), the low angle of the sun brings out the richness of the rocks' colors—especially the reds and oranges—and emphasizes shadows, creating a multidimensional scene. On the other hand, around noon, with light coming straight down, the hoodoos look washed out and flat.

Choosing a location isn't difficult. There are plenty of spots along the Rim Trail for early morning shots; those looking for sunset photos should head down the Rim Trail past Inspiration Point, where it climbs a small hill, for the best angles. Those with telephoto or zoom lenses have the advantage of being able to get a variety of shots from one location along the rim; for close-ups and unique angles, you'll want to hike below the rim, and a wide-angle lens will often produce the best results. Some photographers like to use polarizing filters to bring out the colors of the rocks and deepen the blue of the sky.

A tripod is useful, especially when the light is a bit dim, to minimize vibration and help keep the camera from moving while you find the right composition. Those without tripods can steady their cameras by folding or balling up a jacket or sweater, resting it on a railing or other solid object, and holding the camera against it.

rional and vault toilets toward the Bryce Point end of the loop. The park's horseback ride concessionaire uses the trail spring through fall, and hikers should step aside to let horseback riders through. Hiking the entire trail takes 3 to 4 hours.

6.8 miles RT. Difficult. Access: The trail head is located at the Bryce Point Overlook parking area.

Rim Trail ★★★ _Kids_   The Rim Trail, which does not drop into the canyon but offers splendid views from above, meanders along the rim with a total elevation change of 550 feet. This is more of a walk than a hike, and includes a half-mile section between two overlooks—Sunrise and Sunset—that is suitable for wheelchairs. Overlooking Bryce Amphitheater, the trail offers excellent views almost everywhere and is a good choice for an early morning or

---

(*Tips* **Beating the Heat**

The lower you drop below the rim, the hotter it gets; so carry water and dress in layers that can be easily removed and carried as the temperature rises.

---

evening walk, when you can watch the changing light on the rosy rocks below. Another advantage is that you can access the trail from many locations, so you can have a short or long walk. You may also find this a convenient trail if you just want to rush out to the rim for a quick look at sunrise over the hoodoos. Some feel the absolutely best view in the park is from the Rim Trail, south of Inspiration Point. If you do the whole thing, it's a maximum of 5 to 6 hours.

11 miles RT. Easy to moderate. Access: The N. Trail Head is at Fairyland Point, the S. Trail Head is at Bryce Point. The trail is also accessible from Sunrise, Sunset, and Inspiration points, and numerous other locations in between.

Sheep Creek Trail   This trail takes you down into the canyon bottoms, and if you continue, right out of the park into the Dixie National Forest. The first mile is on the rim, then the trail descends along Sheep Creek draw, below pink limestone cliffs toward the canyon bottom, traversing part of the Under the Rim Trail along its way. Watch signs carefully; the route can be confusing. The trail has up to a 1,250-foot elevation change, and it will take you about 5 hours if you go just to the park boundary, 8 hours if you go to the end.

6–10 miles RT (3 miles takes you to the park boundary and another 2 miles brings you to the national forest boundary). Easy to moderate. Access: The trail head sign and parking area are 5 miles south of the visitor center on the scenic drive.

2 Exploring the Backcountry

For diehard hikers who don't mind rough terrain, Bryce has two backcountry trails, usually open in the summer only. The really ambitious can combine the two for a week-long excursion. Permits, which cost $5 and are available at the visitor center, are required for all overnight trips into the backcountry. These permits cannot be reserved, but are obtained for that day or the following day. Although the number of permits issued is limited, park officials say they seldom run out. Permits can be obtained daily from 8am until 2 hours before the visitor center closes.

Riggs Spring Loop Trail ★★ This hike can be completed in 4 or 5 rigorous hours, or it can be more comfortably done as a relaxing overnight backpacking trip. This relatively little-used trail offers a good opportunity to escape humanity, plus the chance of seeing wildlife, possibly even a glimpse of an elusive mountain lion (see chapter 10, "A Nature Guide to Zion & Bryce Canyon National Parks"). The trail goes through a deep forest of Douglas fir and ponderosa pine early on, and then turns south through a burned-out area, past blackened trees and brush to the brink of the Pink Cliffs, where you can gaze into a valley of hoodoos below. Yovimpa Pass Campground, about 2 miles into the hike, occupies a tree-rimmed meadow with views of Molly's Nipple and No Man's Mesa. The descent from Yovimpa Pass follows the bed of Podunk Creek, crossing the wash several times, and traversing a forest of ponderosa and piñon pines, aspen, Douglas fir, and manzanita, before turning toward Riggs Spring and the Riggs Spring Campground (3.4 miles from the trail head). The spring is on the west side of the trail and encircled by a wood rail fence. The trail next turns north, following Mutton Hollow and crossing several washes, finally arriving at Corral Hollow Campground at the base of the Promontory, just beyond a small stand of maple trees. (You've come 5.7 miles at this point.) The trail now begins the loop around the Promontory, sometimes crossing draws that provide clear views of the white and pink cliffs soaring above. Once around the southern tip of the promontory, the trail begins the steady return ascent to the rim of the canyon. The elevation change of the hike is 1,675 feet.

8.8 miles RT. Moderate to difficult. Access: The trail head is located on the south side of the parking area for Rainbow Point.

Under the Rim Trail Running just below the rim between Bryce and Rainbow points, the Under the Rim Trail has numerous, fairly steep inclines and descents, with an overall elevation change of 1,500 feet. There are five camping areas along the route, plus a group camp area. Doing this whole trail should take you 2 to 3 days.

Although the trail doesn't move too far from the scenic drive, its location below the rim gives hikers a feeling of being alone in the wilderness. There are several spurs connecting this trail to the scenic drive, which enables hikers to choose a route to match their abilities and time schedule. The **Sheep Creek Trail** (9.5 miles from the trail head) and **Swamp Canyon Connecting Trail** (10.4 miles from the trail head) both lead to the Swamp Canyon Overlook and parking area on the scenic drive. **Whiteman Connecting Trail** (12.3 miles from the trail head) takes hikers to a picnic area on the scenic drive; and **Agua Canyon Connecting Trail** (16.9 miles from the trail head) connects to Ponderosa Canyon Overlook and parking area on the scenic drive. However, plan carefully, because once you determine your route it is written on your overnight pass, and you cannot change your campsite.

From Bryce Point, the trail meanders toward Merrell Hollow across almost empty meadows with an occasional twisted conifer and a few manzanita. Nearing the hollow you'll see chipmunks darting about gathering food, and you'll have grand vistas of the Aquarius Plateau, with Tropic Valley nestled in the foreground. The pinnacles grouped at the head of the hollow are brilliantly painted in purples, reds, and oranges. As you descend a long slope, you'll see the Hat Shop ahead (see "Hat Shop Trail," earlier in this chapter); continuing the descent you'll finally arrive at Right Fork Camping Area (3 miles from the trail head) located in a tall stand of ponderosa pines.

From Right Fork, the trail follows a deep wash through low brush to Yellow Creek, which it follows upstream, passing the Yellow Creek Group Camp (4 miles from the trail head). As you continue upstream, you'll pass desert shrubs and barrel cactus among the junipers (see chapter 10, "A Nature Guide to Zion & Bryce Canyon National Parks"), and in the occasional spaces between the trees you can see the colorful spires at the top of the valley. Near the stream source is the Yellow Creek Camping Area (5.4 miles from the trail head) in a grove of tall pines; shortly after you leave the campground the trail climbs a slope with grand views to the east, where gray cliffs provide a backdrop for deep red formations of sandstone.

The trail next passes through open pine forests, along washes, and up and down valleys, offering varying views of carved and etched walls, square-topped pillars, and a mountain topped with sharp pinnacles. Rock cairns mark the trail when it begins to fade. Once across the Sheep Creek Trail and wash, you'll wind around, up, and then down into the Swamp Canyon bottoms, where cool air pools and aspens grow. After the Right Fork Swamp Canyon Camp (10.5 miles from the trail head), you'll climb onto the top of the plateau, pass an amphitheater filled with lovely hoodoos, and arrive at Swamp Canyon Camp (12.2 miles from the trail head), high above the canyon floor.

As you continue, the trail heads in a southerly direction, descending into the upper basin of Willis Creek, climbing into a sandy saddle, and then descending into Bridge Canyon—look to the west for a clear view of Natural Bridge. Once in the canyon bottom the trail arrives at Bridge Canyon Camp (15.6 miles from the trail head), nestled among pine trees. Although cliffs are visible from the campground, the Natural Bridge is blocked from view.

After crossing an open meadow that's blanketed with a profusion of yellow wildflowers in late summer, you'll follow Agua Canyon upstream—rock cairns help keep you on course. As you approach the head of the wash, you'll start up a steep, north-facing incline partially shaded with Douglas fir. As you near the crest, the trees thin out, providing magnificent views north and west.

Dropping into the next basin, you pass under a colorful cliff, after which the trail climbs several ridges and skirts a bowl filled with hoodoos, before arriving at the small Iron Spring Camping Area (19½ miles from the trail head). Next you'll climb a gradual but constant slope toward the rim, with increasingly panoramic views of the orange cliffs north to Bryce Point. Soon a turn to the west blocks this vista, and you have a steep climb to achieve the rim and the Rainbow Point parking area, the end of the trail, where you'll find a picnic area and restrooms. Rainbow Point is also the trail head for the Bristlecone Loop and Riggs Spring Loop trails (see above).

22.6 miles one-way. Moderately strenuous. Access: The trail head is located on the east side of the parking area for Bryce Point Overlook.

3 Other Summer Sports & Activities

BIKING   Bikes are prohibited on all trails, as well as forbidden from traveling cross-country within the national park boundaries. This leaves the park's established scenic drive, which is open to road or mountain bikers, although you need to be aware that the 18-mile road through the park is narrow and winding, and can be crowded with motor vehicles during the summer.

Because mountain bikers are not welcome on national park hiking trails, you'll have to leave Bryce in search of trails. Fortunately, you won't have to go far—the **Dixie National Forest,** which abuts the park, has numerous mountain biking opportunities (see chapter 9, "Nearby Things to See & Do").

FISHING   The closest fishing hole to the park is at **Tropic Reservoir** in the Dixie National Forest (see chapter 9, "Nearby Things to See & Do").

HORSEBACK RIDING   To see Bryce Canyon the way early pioneers did, you need to look down from a horse or mule. **Canyon Trail Rides,** P.O. Box 128, Tropic, UT 84776 (✆ **435/679-8665;**

fax 435/679-8709; www.onpages.com/canyonrides), offers a close-up view of Bryce's spectacular rock formations from the relative comfort of a saddle, and welcomes first-time riders. They have a desk inside Bryce Lodge. A 2-hour ride to the canyon floor and back costs $30, including tax, per person, and a half-day trip farther into the canyon costs $45 per person. Rides are offered, weather permitting, April through November.

Guided rides are also provided by **Ruby's Scenic Rim and Outlaw Trail Rides** (© **800/679-5859** or 435/834-5280), at Ruby's Inn, at similar rates; in addition, Ruby's offers a full-day ride with lunch for $75. There are age and weight limits, and reservations are recommended for both companies. Ruby's will also board your horse (call for rates).

4 Winter Activities

Bryce is beautiful in the winter when the white snow creates a perfect frosting on the red, pink, orange, and brown statues standing proudly against the cold winds.

CROSS-COUNTRY SKIING Cross-country skiers will find several marked, ungroomed trails (all above the rim), including the **Fairyland Loop Trail** 🌟🌟, which leads 1 mile through a pine and juniper forest to the Fairyland Point Overlook. From here you can take the 1-mile **Forest Trail** back to the road, or continue north along the rim for another 1.2 miles to the park boundary.

There are also connections to ski trails in the adjacent national forest (see "Dixie National Forest" in chapter 9).

Stop at the visitor center for additional trail information, and go to **Best Western Ruby's Inn,** just north of the park entrance (© **435/834-5341;** see chapter 9, "Nearby Things to See & Do"), for information on cross-country ski trails and snowmobiling opportunities outside the park. Ruby's grooms over 30 miles (50km) of ski trails, and also rents cross-country ski equipment.

SNOWSHOEING Snowshoeing is allowed anywhere in the park except on cross-country ski tracks.

Tips Winter Safety

Although the entire park is open to cross-country skiers, rangers warn that it's extremely dangerous to try to ski on the steep—and often slick—trails leading down into the canyon.

8

Where to Stay, Camp & Eat in Bryce Canyon

Although you don't have as many choices for lodging, dining, and camping inside the park as you do at larger national parks, to our thinking, what is offered at Bryce Canyon is a perfect compliment to your national park experience. In addition to being well managed, the Bryce Canyon Lodge and park campgrounds, offer incredible views and a rustic, rugged, mountain atmosphere that can't be beat.

However, let's not put down the facilities available in the nearby gateway communities. Here you'll find a variety of lodging and dining choices, often at lower prices than inside the park, as well as campgrounds with RV hookups and all the other amenities that are lacking in the national park campgrounds.

1 Where to Stay

Room tax adds about 9% to your lodging bill. Pets are not accepted unless otherwise noted.

INSIDE THE PARK

Bryce Canyon Lodge ☆☆☆ This sandstone and ponderosa pine lodge, which opened in 1924, is the perfect place to stay while exploring Bryce Canyon National Park. Its location, near the Rim Trail, is ideal for watching the play of changing light on the rock formations at various times of the day.

Guests can choose from three types of accommodations. The luxurious lodge suites are wonderful, with white wicker furniture, ceiling fans, and separate sitting rooms. The motel units are simply pleasant, modern motel rooms, with two queen-size beds and either a balcony or patio. What you're paying for here is location. Our choice is one of the historic cabins, restored to their 1920s appearance. They're not large, but have two double beds, high ceilings, stone (gas-burning) fireplaces, and log beams—you might call the ambience "rustic luxury." The gift shop has one of the best selections of American Indian pawn jewelry in the area, and of course a variety of postcards and souvenirs. Try to reserve 4 to 6 months in advance.

Bryce Canyon National Park, UT. © **435/834-5361**. Information and reservations: Amfac Parks & Resorts, 14001 E. Iliff Ave., Suite 600, Aurora, CO 80014. © **303/ 297-2757**. Fax 303/297-3175. www.brycecanyonlodge.com. 114 units in motel rooms and cabins; 3 suites and 1 studio in lodge. $93–$99 motel double; $103–$108 cabin; $123–$129 lodge unit. AE, DISC, MC, V. Closed Nov–Mar. **Amenities:** Restaurant (see "Where to Eat," later in this chapter); activities desk.

OUTSIDE THE PARK
TROPIC & BRYCE

See chapter 9, "Nearby Things to See & Do," for a discussion of things to see and do in these gateway communities, and for additional information, contact **Bryce Canyon Country** (the Garfield County Travel Council), P.O. Box 200, Panguitch, UT 84759 (© **800/444-6689** or 435/676-1160; fax 435/676-8239; www. brycecanyoncountry.com).

Best Western Ruby's Inn 🐾🐾 *Kids*   Most of the tired hikers and canyon rim gazers visiting Bryce Canyon National Park stay at this large Best Western, and with good reason—this is where practically everything is happening. The lobby, with a stone fireplace and a western motif of animal head trophies and American Indian blankets, is among the busiest places in the area. It boasts tour desks where you can arrange excursions of all sorts, from horseback and all-terrain-vehicle rides to helicopter flights; you're welcome to stop by and schedule activities even if you're not staying at the hotel.

Spread among nine buildings, the modern motel rooms contain art depicting scenes of the area, wood furnishings, and shower/tub combos. Some have whirlpool tubs. Rooms at the back of the complex will be a bit quieter, but farther from the lobby.

Utah 63 at the entrance to Bryce Canyon (P.O. Box 1), Bryce, UT 84764. © **800/ 468-8660** or 435/834-5341. Fax 435/834-5265. www.rubysinn.com. 369 units, including 60 suites. June–Sept $95–$110 double, $135 suite; Apr–May and Oct $66–$87 double, $115 suite; Nov–Mar $46–$63 double, $85 suite. AE, DC, DISC, MC, V. Pets accepted. **Amenities:** Restaurant (see "Where to Eat," later in this chapter); 2 indoor pools; 1 indoor and 1 outdoor whirlpool; cross-country ski trails; game room; concierge; courtesy transportation from the Bryce Airport; car-rental desk; business center; salon; 1-hour film processor; ATM; western art gallery; huge general store; small liquor store; 2 coin-op laundries; U.S. Post Office; 2 gas stations. *In room:* A/C, TV.

Bryce Canyon Pines   A modern motel with a western flair, the Bryce Canyon Pines offers well-maintained rooms with light-colored wood furnishings and two queen-size beds in most rooms.

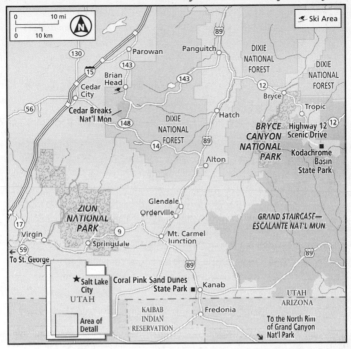

Some units have fireplaces (wood supplied free), some have fully-stocked kitchenettes, and one has its own whirlpool tub. You can also book horseback rides from Red Canyon Trail Rides (see "Dixie National Forest" in chapter 9) and trail ride/lodging packages.

Utah 12 (3 miles west of intersection with park entry road; P.O. Box 64000-43), Bryce, UT 84764. © **800/892-7923** or 435/834-5441. Fax 435/834-5330. www.brycecanyonmotel.com. 51 units. Summer, $65–$85 double; $95–$125 kitchenettes and suites. Lower rates in winter. AE, DC, DISC, MC, V. **Amenities:** Restaurant adjacent (see "Where to Eat," later in this chapter); covered heated pool. *In room:* A/C, TV.

Bryce Canyon Resorts ★★ This attractive property is a somewhat elegant change-of-pace from the western and Southwest decor found in most other lodgings in the area. It also has a good location, adjacent to the main parking area for the Bryce Canyon shuttle, at the intersection of Utah Highways 12 and 63.

The spacious rooms are Victorian in style, with drapes and bed coverings in royal purples and reds, and solid wood furniture stained a rich mahogany. Each contains one king- or two queen-size beds, a table and chairs, two sinks, a shower-tub combo, and an ample closet. There are also some renovated historic cabins (which do not have A/C), and cottages with kitchenettes. There's also a campground.

13500 E. Utah 12 (P.O. Box 640006), Bryce, UT 84764. © **800/834-0043** or 435/834-5351. Fax 435/834-5256. www.brycecanyonresorts.com. 70 units. Summer, $50–$85 double; $95 kitchenette units. Lower rates at other times. MC, V. Small pets accepted for a $5 fee. **Amenities:** Restaurant; outdoor pool; sauna. *In room:* A/C, TV.

Bryce Country Cabins 🔊

There's something neat about staying in a cabin during a national park vacation, but there's also something very appealing about hot showers and warm beds. Bryce Country cabins offers both, with six recently-constructed log-style cabins and a historic two-room pioneer cottage, set on a 20-acre farm. The grounds surrounding the cabins and cottage are nicely landscaped, and you get views out over the national park, although we wish the units were further back from the highway. The intriguing part of the facility, though, is the farm behind the buildings, where cattle graze in the fields and the chickens think they own the place.

The comfortable cabins have knotty pine walls and ceilings, exposed beams, and ceiling fans. Each has two queen-size beds, a table with two chairs, and a private porch. Bathrooms have showers only. The cottage, built in 1905, has two spacious rooms with country-style decor, each with its own entrance. Both have two queen-size beds and full bathrooms with shower/tub combos. The cottage's two rooms can be rented together or individually.

320 N. Utah 12 (P.O. Box 141), Tropic, UT 84776. © **888/679-8643** or 435/679-8643. Fax 435/679-8989. www.brycecountrycabins.com. 8 units. Summer, $65–$75 double; lower rates at other times. DC, MC, V. *In room:* A/C, TV, coffeemaker.

Bryce Pioneer Village

This is a good choice for those seeking a good night's rest at a reasonable rate. The small, no-frills motel rooms have showers only (no tubs) but they're clean, comfortable, and have fairly large walk-in closets. Cabins, which were relocated from inside the national park, are more interesting. Most are small but cute, with one queen bed plus a twin bed, one chair, and a small bathroom with a shower (no tub). Several others, which have been renovated within the past few years, are much larger, with two queen beds, and average-size bathrooms with shower/tub combinations. There are also two rooms with three queen beds each. Just outside the motel office, you can see the cabin where Ebenezer and Mary Bryce, for whom the national park is named, lived in the late 1870s.

80 S. Main St. (Utah 12; P.O. Box 119), Tropic, UT 84776. ℂ **800/222-0381** or 435/679-8546. Fax 435/679-8607. www.bpvillage.com. 69 units. $55–$75 double; $55–$85 cabins and kitchenette units. AE, MC, V. Pets accepted in cabins. Closed Nov–Mar. **Amenities:** 2 hot tubs; picnic area. *In room:* A/C, TV.

Bryce Point Bed & Breakfast ⚜   Lamar and Ethel LeFevre have named and decorated each room in their bed-and-breakfast for one of their children. For instance, son Les is a firefighter, so the Les and Dela room contains fire-fighting memorabilia and photos. The decor is tasteful and not overdone, and most rooms offer beautiful views of Bryce Point through large picture windows. All rooms have queen or king beds and private bathrooms (showers only). The honeymoon cottage is beautifully furnished in country style, with a gas fireplace in the living room, full kitchen, washer and dryer, and a king bed in the spacious bedroom. Breakfasts are full, satisfying, and homemade, with selections such as bacon and eggs with pancakes and apple cider syrup. The B&B is entirely no-smoking.

61 N. 400 W. (P.O. Box 96), Tropic, UT 84776-0096. ℂ **888/200-4211** or 435/679-8629 (voice/fax). 6 units. $70 double; $90–$120 honeymoon cottage. Rates include full breakfast. MC, V. **Amenities:** Large enclosed hot tub. *In room:* TV/VCR, free use of the LeFevre's video collection, no phone.

Bryce View Lodge ⚜ *Value*   This basic modern American motel gets our vote for the best combination of economy and location. It consists of four two-story buildings, set back from the road and grouped around a large parking lot and attractively landscaped area. Rooms are simple but comfortable, recently refurbished, and are quite quiet. Guests have access to the amenities across the street at Ruby's Inn.

Utah 63 across from Best Western Ruby's Inn (P.O. Box 64002), Bryce, UT 84764. ℂ **888/279-2304** or 435/834-5180. Fax 435/834-5181. www.bryceviewlodge. com. 160 units. $44–$60 double. AE, DC, DISC, MC, V. Pets accepted. **Amenities:** See Ruby's Inn above. *In room:* A/C, TV.

Canyon Livery Bed & Breakfast   The simply decorated rooms in this delightful bed-and-breakfast have beautiful handmade quilts on the queen beds. Two are dedicated to women pioneers and have brass beds, two have handmade wooden beds and are dedicated to male pioneers. The fifth is western, with a wonderful high arched window providing terrific views of the night sky. Breakfasts include a hot dish, homemade breads, fresh fruits (often from the B&B's

own trees), juices, and coffee. All rooms have windows facing the national park, and the three upstairs rooms have private balconies. There is a corral if you have a horse with you ($5 a day extra, plus food). Smoking is not permitted.

50 S. 660 W. (P.O. Box 24), Tropic, UT 84776-0024. ℂ **888/889-8910** or 435/679-8780. Call for fax. www.canyonlivery.com. 5 units. Apr–Oct $75–$95 double; Nov–Mar $65–$75 double. Rates include full breakfast. MC, V. *In room:* A/C, no phone.

Foster's   Clean and economical lodging is what you'll find at Foster's. A modular unit contains small rooms, each with either one queen-size or two double beds, and decorated with posters showing scenery of the area; bathrooms have showers only. Also on the grounds is a grocery store (open 7am–10pm, closed Oct–Feb) with a rather nice bakery.

Utah 12 (mailing address: Star Route, Panguitch, UT 84759), Bryce, UT. ℂ **800/ 372-4750** or 435/834-5227. Fax 435/834-5304. 52 units. Summer $50 double; winter $40 double. AE, DISC, MC, V. 1½ miles west of the national park access road turnoff. **Amenities:** Restaurant (see "Where to Eat," later in this chapter). *In room:* A/C, TV.

World Host Bryce Valley Inn   These simply decorated, basic motel rooms offer a clean, economical choice for park visitors. Rooms, all of which have shower/tub combos, are furnished with either one or two queen beds. There's one suite with two queens and a hide-a-bed. A gift shop on the premises offers a large selection of American Indian arts and crafts, handmade gifts, rocks, and fossils.

199 N. Main St., Tropic, UT 84776. ℂ **800/442-1890** or 435/679-8811. Fax 435/679-8846. www.brycevalleyinn.com. 65 units. Apr–Oct $55–$65 double; Nov–Mar $35–$45 double. AE, DISC, MC, V. 8 miles east of the park entrance road. Pets accepted for a fee. **Amenities:** Restaurant (see "Where to Eat," later in this chapter); 24-hr. coin-operated laundry. *In room:* A/C, TV.

2 Camping

Pets are accepted at all the following campgrounds but must be leashed.

INSIDE THE PARK

The two campgrounds at Bryce are typical of the West's national parks. Campers get easy access to trails and plenty of trees, but limited facilities. **North Campground** ⋆⋆⋆ has 105 sites and **Sunset Campground** ⋆⋆ has 111 sites. Sunset Campground is open May through September only, but a section of North Campground is open year-round. North Campground is also closer to the Rim Trail, making it easier to rush over to catch those amazing sunrise and sunset colors. Get to the park early to claim a site (usually by 2pm in the summer).

Showers ($2) and a coin-operated laundry, open from 7am to 8pm, are located at the **General Store** (for information, contact Bryce Canyon Lodge ℂ **435/834-5361**), although it's a healthy walk from either campground. The park service operates an RV dump station ($2 fee) in the summer.

OUTSIDE THE PARK

Just north of the entrance to the park is **Ruby's Inn RV Park & Campground** &&, Utah 63 (P.O. Box 22), Bryce, UT 84764 (ℂ **800/468-8660** or 435/834-5301, Nov–Mar 435/834-5341; fax 435/834-5481; www.rubysinn.com), along the park's shuttle bus route. Both RV and tent sites are mostly shady and attractive. The campground contains a game room, horseshoes, a swimming pool, barbecue grills, two coin-op laundries, and a store with groceries and RV supplies. A lake and a horse pasture are nearby.

Bryce Canyon Resorts, at the junction of Utah Highways 12 and 63 (P.O. Box 640006), Bryce, UT 84764 (ℂ **800/834-0043** or 435/834-5351; fax 435/834-5256; www.brycecanyonresorts.com), offers convenient tent and RV campsites, within easy walking distance of the main boarding area for the Bryce Canyon Shuttle. There's some grass and a tree or two, and additional landscaping is planned. There's also a motel and restaurant on the property.

Bryce Pioneer Village, 80 S. Main St. (Utah 12; P.O. Box 119), Tropic, UT 84776 (ℂ **800/222-0381** or 435/679-8546; fax 435/679-8607; www.bpvillage.com), is a small motel/cabins/campground combination in nearby Tropic, with some shade trees and easy access to several restaurants. Dump-station use costs $3. Showers are available to noncampers for $2.

Bryce Canyon Pines &, milepost 10, Utah 12 (P.O. Box 64000-435), Bryce, UT 84764 (ℂ **800/892-7923** or 435/834-5441; fax 435/834-5330; www.brycecanyonmotel.com), is part of a motel/restaurant/store/campground complex about 3½ miles west of the park entrance road. The campsites, set back from the highway behind a gas station and store, are interspersed among ponderosa pines and junipers, with wildflowers and grasses. Campers have access to the motel swimming pool across the street. Those not camping here can get showers for $2.50.

Amenities for Each Campground, Bryce Canyon National Park

Campground	Elev.	Total Sites	RV Hookups	Dump Station	Toilets	Drinking Water	Showers	Fire Pits/ Grills	Public Phone	Laundry	Reserve	Fees	Open
North	7,700	105	no	no	yes	yes	no	yes	no	no	no	$10	Year-round
Sunset	8,000	111	no	no	yes	yes	no	yes	no	no	no	$10	May–Sept
Bryce Canyon Pines	7,600	39	26	no	yes	yes	yes	yes	yes	yes	yes	$16–$22	Mar–Nov
Bryce Canyon Resort	7,650	44	24	no	yes	yes	yes	no	yes	yes	yes	$15–$25	Apr–Oct
Bryce Pioneer Village	7,600	15	15	yes	yes	yes	yes	no	no	no	yes	$10–$15	Mid-Apr to Oct
King's Creek (USFS)	8,000	34	no	yes	yes	yes	no	yes	no	no	no	$8	Mem. Day to Labor Day
Red Canyon (USFS)	7,400	37	no	yes	yes	yes	yes	yes	no	no	no	$9	Apr–Oct
Ruby's Inn RV Park	7,600	227	127	yes	yes	yes	yes	yes	yes	yes	yes	$16–$25	Apr–Oct
Kodachrome	5,800	24	no	yes	yes	yes	yes	yes	no	yes	yes	$13	Year-round

King's Creek Campground, in the Dixie National Forest (mailing address 82 N. 100 E., Cedar City, UT 84720; © **435/ 865-3700;** www.fs.fed.us/dxnf), above Tropic Reservoir, has graded gravel roads and sites nestled among tall ponderosa pines. The nearby reservoir has two boat ramps (see "Dixie National Forest" in chapter 9, "Nearby Things to See & Do"). To get to the campground from the park, head north 3 miles on Utah 63, then west on Utah 12 about 2½ miles to the access road, turn south (left) and follow signs to Tropic Reservoir for about 7 miles to the campground.

About 9½ miles west of the park is another Dixie National Forest campground, **Red Canyon Campground** (same contact as King's Creek Campground, above). Nestled among the trees along the south side of Utah 12, it offers terrific views of the red rock formations across the highway, although there is a bit of road noise. Showers cost $2, whether you're staying in the campground or not.

Kodachrome Basin State Park (see chapter 9, "Nearby Things to See & Do"), about 22 miles southeast of the park, has an attractive campground with sites scattered among unusual rock "chimneys" and piñon and juniper trees.

3 Where to Eat

INSIDE THE PARK

Picnickers can stock up at the small General Store inside the park or at one of several stores not far from the park entrance. See the Fast Facts entry for "Supplies" in chapter 6, "Exploring Bryce Canyon National Park."

Bryce Canyon Lodge AMERICAN   The dining room is delightful: the quintessential mountain lodge, with two large stone fireplaces, American Indian weavings and baskets, a huge 45-star 1897 American flag, and large windows that provide wonderful views. But the food's good, too—and quite reasonably priced considering that this is the only real restaurant in the park. The menu is subject to change, but at dinner it's likely to include excellent slow-roasted prime rib au jus and fresh mountain trout. There are usually several vegetarian items also available, such as lasagna or black bean stuffed peppers. The lodge's specialty ice creams and desserts include the exotic (and very tasty) wild "Bryceberry" bread pudding and the excellent caramel apple cheesecake. At lunch you'll find the trout, plus burgers, sandwiches, stew, and salads. All the usual American selections are offered for breakfast, and an excellent breakfast buffet is usually available. The restaurant will pack lunches to go, and offers full liquor service.

Bryce Canyon National Park. © **435/834-5361.** www.brycecanyonlodge.com. Reservations required for dinner. Breakfast $3.75–$9.25; lunch $4.95–$10.95; dinner $10.50–$19.95. AE, DC, DISC, MC, V. Daily 6:30am–4:30pm and 5:30–9:30pm. Closed Nov–Mar.

OUTSIDE THE PARK
TROPIC & BRYCE

Bryce Canyon Pines *Finds* AMERICAN   A country cottage-style dining room, with an old wood stove, is a good setting for the wholesome American food served here. Especially popular for its traditional breakfasts, the restaurant is also known for its homemade soups and pies. Both sandwiches and full dinners are available at lunch and dinner. Recommended are the hot sandwiches, such as the open-faced turkey with mashed potatoes and gravy; the Utah trout; and the 8-ounce tenderloin steak. Beer and wine are available.

Utah 12 about 3 miles west of intersection with park entry road. © **435/ 834-5441.** www.brycecanyonmotel.com. Sandwiches $3.95–$7.95; full dinners $9.95–$17.50. AE, DC, DISC, MC, V. Daily 6:30am–9:30pm (may close slightly earlier in spring and fall). Closed mid-Nov to mid-Mar.

Canyon Diner *Kids* AMERICAN   Part of the Ruby's Inn complex, this fast-food restaurant is a great place to fill up the kids without going broke. Breakfasts, served until 11am, include bagels and several egg croissants; for lunch and dinner, you can get hoagies, burgers, hot dogs, particularly good stuffed potatoes, fresh-made pizza, broiled chicken sandwiches, and salads. We especially recommend the Piccadilly (English-style) chips. Specialties include bratwurst with homemade sauerkraut and a halibut fish-and-chips basket. No alcohol is served.

Just north of the park entrance on Utah 63, at Ruby's Inn, Bryce. © **435/834-5341.** www.rubysinn.com. Reservations not accepted. Individual items $2–$5; meals $4–$8.50. AE, DISC, MC, V. Daily 6:30am–10pm. Closed Nov–Mar.

Foster's Family Steak House STEAK/SEAFOOD   The simple western decor here provides the appropriate atmosphere for a family steakhouse, popular among locals for its slow-roasted prime rib and steamed Utah trout. Foster's also offers several steaks, including a 14-ounce T-bone, sandwiches, a soup of the day, and homemade western-style chile with beans. All the pastries, pies, and breads are baked on the premises. Bottled beer is served.

Utah 12 about 1½ miles west of the park entrance road. © **435/834-5227.** Reservations not accepted. Breakfast and lunch items $1.75–$6; main dinner courses $9–$19. AE, DISC, MC, V. Mar–Nov daily 7am–10pm; Dec–Feb daily 4–10pm.

Doug's Place Restaurant STEAK/SEAFOOD This family steakhouse, with a decidedly western atmosphere, specializes in innovative twists on American standards, such as a 10-ounce choice sirloin, marinated in a lime sauce and flame broiled; and Cajun-style blackened rainbow trout, pan fried. The dinner menu also includes simply prepared charbroiled steaks, pan-fried salmon and fresh rainbow trout, Texas-style barbecue, chicken, and pork chops. You'll find traditional American breakfasts—try the pancakes—and burgers and sandwiches at lunch. Beer is available.

141 N. Main St., Tropic. ✆ **435/679-8633**. www.dougsplace.net. Lunch $3.95–$6.95; dinner $10.45–$16.95. AE, DISC, MC, V. Daily 6:30am–10pm. Closed Nov–Feb.

Hungry Coyote Restaurant & Saloon AMERICAN/WESTERN Rough wood walls, kerosene lanterns, and warnings that patrons must "check your gun with the waitress" all contribute to the Old West atmosphere. Beef lovers will savor the thick 20-ounce T-bone, the most expensive item on the menu; also popular is the local trout. Other choices include pork chops and grilled chicken breast. The restaurant offers full liquor service.

199 N. Main St. at the World Host Bryce Valley Inn, Tropic. ✆ **435/679-8822**. www.brycevalleyinn.com. Breakfast $3.95–$6.95; dinner main courses $6–$21. AE, DISC, MC, V. Daily 6–11am and 5–10pm; reduced hours in winter.

Ruby's Inn Cowboy's Buffet and Steak Room STEAK/ SEAFOOD The busiest restaurant in the Bryce Canyon area, Ruby's moves 'em through with buffets at every meal, plus a well-rounded menu and friendly service. The breakfast buffet offers more choices than you'd expect, with scrambled eggs, fresh fruit, several breakfast meats, potatoes, pastries, and cereals. At the lunch buffet, you'll find country-style ribs, fresh fruit, salads, soups, vegetables, and breads; while the dinner buffet features charbroiled thin-sliced rib eye steak and other meats, pastas, potatoes, and salads. Regular menu dinner entrees include prime rib, slow roasted baby back ribs, breaded-and-grilled southern Utah rainbow trout, broiled chicken breast, burgers, and salads. In addition to the large, western-style dining room, an outdoor patio is open in good weather. Full liquor service is available.

Utah 63, the Ruby's Inn complex, Bryce. ✆ **435/834-5341**. www.rubysinn.com. Reservations not accepted. Buffets: breakfast $8.50 adults, $6 children 3–12; lunch $9 and $7; dinner $14.50 and $7.50. Main courses $3.50–$13.95 breakfast and lunch, $5.50–$19.95 dinner. AE, DC, DISC, MC, V. Summer daily 6:30am–10pm; winter daily 6:30am–9pm.

9

Nearby Things to See & Do

The area surrounding Zion and Bryce Canyon National Parks offers a smorgasbord of scenic wonders and recreational opportunities. The gateway communities to the parks offer a variety of activities and often provide a welcome change of pace for kids who might be getting a bit tired of the beautiful but seemingly endless rock formations. Adjacent to Bryce Canyon National Park is Grand Staircase–Escalante—a vast, new, stunning national monument—as well as Dixie National Forest, a popular spot for mountain bikers. Within 90 minutes of the south entrance to Zion National Park, you can wander through the mysterious lava caves of Snow Canyon, or strike out off-road in a dune buggy at Coral Pink Sand Dunes State Park—and that's just for starters. Two other state parks, Kodachrome Basin and Escalante, are within an hour of the entrance to Bryce Canyon and provide lovely vistas and quirky pleasures all their own. In addition to the telephone numbers listed below, you can get information on the state parks discussed in this chapter online at **http://parks.state.ut.us**.

1 Gateway Towns

Just outside the parks are communities offering additional outdoor recreation opportunities. Additional information is provided in the chapters covering activities in each of the parks.

OUTSIDE ZION NATIONAL PARK

The small community of **Springdale**, population about 350 and an elevation of 3,800 feet, was settled in 1862 and today is the south gateway to Zion National Park. This is also a good spot to pick up those forgotten supplies.

The community of **Virgin** (pop. 375) lies about 13 miles west of Springdale along Utah 9. First named Pocketville because of the closeness of the surrounding red sandstone cliffs, the town was renamed for the Virgin River that runs through it. The Kolob Terrace Road heads north out of Virgin into Zion National Park, accessing several backcountry trails.

✒ How's This for Gun Control?

In response to fears that the right of U.S. citizens to own firearms was under attack, the small town of Virgin, Utah, about 15 miles west of the main entrance to Zion National Park, has passed a law that requires—that's REQUIRES—that there be a gun and ammunition in every home. The ordinance, approved in late 2000, exempts residents who cannot afford to buy a gun or have moral objections, as well as those who are mentally ill or convicted felons. The town's mayor said there was a lot of support from the town's 350 residents, most of whom already owned guns.

For additional information about the area contact the **Zion Canyon Chamber of Commerce,** P.O. Box 331, Springdale, UT 84767-0331 (✆ **888/518-7070;** www.zionpark.com); or **Utah's Southwest Color Country,** P.O. Box 1550, St. George, UT 84771-1550 (✆ **800/233-8824** or 435/628-4171; fax 435/673-3540; www.colorcountry.org).

Hiking and mountain biking are popular activities around Springdale. Visit **Bike Zion,** 1458 Zion Park Blvd. (P.O. Box 272), Springdale, UT 84767 (✆ **800/475-4576** or 435/772-3929; www.bikezion.com) for advice, bike rentals, and guided tours (see chapter 4, "Hikes & Other Outdoor Pursuits in Zion National Park").

The **Tanner Summer Series** presents multi-discipline performing arts in the stunning, 2000-seat outdoor **O. C. Tanner Amphitheater,** just off Zion Park Boulevard. Concerts range from symphony orchestra and dance companies to bluegrass and cowboy poetry, begin at 8pm every Saturday from Memorial Day to Labor Day, and cost $8 per person. For information, contact **Dixie College,** in St. George (✆ **435/652-7994**).

The **Zion Canyon Theatre,** 145 Zion Park Blvd. (✆ **435/ 772-2400;** www.zioncanyontheatre.com) boasts a huge screen—some six stories high by 80 feet wide. Here you can see the dramatic film *Zion Canyon—Treasure of the Gods,* with thrilling scenes of the Zion National Park area, including a hair-raising flash flood through Zion Canyon's Narrows and some dizzying bird's-eye views. Admission costs $7.50 adults, $5.50 seniors, $4.50 children 3 to 11, and is free for children under 3. The theater is open daily year-round except Christmas. Shows begin hourly, April through October from 9am to 9pm, and November through March from 11am to 7pm. The theater complex also contains a tourist information center, ATM, picnic area, gift and souvenir shops, deli, ice cream shop, Paiute Indian exhibit, and bookstore.

OUTSIDE BRYCE CANYON NATIONAL PARK

Just outside the entrance to Bryce Canyon National Park are the communities of **Tropic,** along Utah 12 about 8 miles east of the park entrance road, and **Bryce,** along the entrance road and near its intersection with Utah 12. Much of the lodging, dining, and other services for park visitors can be found in these communities.

For visitor information, contact **Bryce Canyon Country** (the Garfield County Travel Council), P.O. Box 200, Panguitch, UT 84759 (© **800/444-6689** or 435/676-1160; fax 435/676-8239; www.brycecanyoncountry.com).

There are a variety of outdoor activities in the Dixie National Forest (see below).

For other diversions, the **Best Western Ruby's Inn** (see "Where to Stay" in chapter 8), is practically a one-stop entertainment center for those looking for a bit of variety in their national park vacation.

Directly across Utah 63 from the motel are **Old Bryce Town Shops,** open from mid-May to September, where you'll find a rock shop, souvenir shops, a Christmas store, and an opportunity to buy that genuine cowboy hat you've been wanting. There's a trail especially for kids where they can search for arrowheads, fossils, and petrified wood; you can also try your hand at panning for gold.

Nearby, **Bryce Canyon Country Rodeo** has bucking broncos, bull riding, calf roping, and all sorts of rodeo fun in a 1-hour program from Memorial Day to August, Monday through Saturday evenings at 7pm. Admission is $7 for adults and $4 for children under 12.

2 Dixie National Forest

ADJACENT TO BRYCE CANYON NATIONAL PARK

The Dixie National Forest wraps around two-thirds of Bryce Canyon National Park: all down the west side, around the south end, and about halfway up the east side. There are a variety of outdoor activities in the forest—hiking, mountain biking, fishing, camping, and cross-country skiing—and one national park trail (Sheep Creek Trail) connects with trails in the national forest. The climate and seasons here are similar to Bryce Canyon National Park (see chapter 2, "Planning Your Trip to Zion & Bryce Canyon National Parks").

JUST THE FACTS

INFORMATION & VISITOR CENTER   Stop at the Dixie National Forest's **Red Canyon Visitor Center** (usually open early May to mid-Oct), along Utah 12 about 10½ miles west of the Bryce Canyon National Park entrance road (© **435/676-2676**); or contact the **Dixie National Forest,** 82 North 100 E., Cedar City, UT 84720 (© **435/865-3700;** www.fs.fed.us/dxnf). The visitor center is open daily from 8am to 6pm.

CAMPING   King's Creek Campground, above Tropic Reservoir, has graded gravel roads and sites nestled among tall ponderosa pines. About 9½ miles west of the park is **Red Canyon Campground,** named for its vermilion-colored rock formations. See listings under "Camping," in chapter 8, "Where to Stay, Camp & Eat at Bryce Canyon."

SPORTS & ACTIVITIES

FISHING   The closest fishing hole to Bryce Canyon National Park is at **Tropic Reservoir,** a large lake in a ponderosa pine forest. From the national park entrance road, drive west about 3 miles on Utah 12 to a gravel road, turn left (south), and go about 7 miles. There is a forest service campground open in the summer, a boat ramp, and fishing for rainbow, brook, and cutthroat trout. Locals say fishing is sometimes better in streams above the lake than in the reservoir itself.

HIKING   There are about a dozen trails in Red Canyon, and a free map is available at forest service offices. Some are open to hikers only; others are open also to mountain bikers, equestrians, and those with all-terrain–vehicles. One especially scenic multi-use trail is the 5.3-mile (one-way) **Casto Canyon Trail,** which runs along the bottom of Casto Canyon. It connects with the 8.7-mile (one-way) **Cassidy Trail** and 3-mile (one-way) **Losee Canyon Trail** to produce a 17-mile loop that is ideal for a backpacking trip of several days. Watch for elk in the winter, and pronghorn antelope and raptors year-round. The Casto Canyon and Losee Canyon trails are considered moderate, while Cassidy Trail ranges from easy to strenuous. **Sheep Creek Trail** (described in chapter 7, "Hikes & Other Outdoor Pursuits in Bryce Canyon National Park") connects the national forest to Bryce Canyon National Park.

For a quick walk, take the half-mile **Pink Ledges Trail,** which is actually a series of short trails that starts just outside the Red

Canyon Visitor Center. Rated moderate because of a few steep inclines, the trail has several signs discussing trees and plants, and good views of surrounding hoodoos. The only downside is that you can't escape the road noise from Utah 12.

HORSEBACK RIDING   If you've brought your own horse, you'll have a number of riding opportunities on the forest's multi-use trails. Those without horses of their own can still explore the canyon on horseback with **Red Canyon Trail Rides** (© **800/ 892-7923** or 435/834-5441), with offices at Bryce Canyon Pines Motel (see "Where to Stay" in chapter 8). Trail rides are offered March through November, weather permitting, with rates of $10 for a half hour, $15 for 1 hour, $35 for a half day, and $85 for a full day, which includes lunch. Minimum age is 6 for the half-hour and hour rides and 7 for the half- and full-day rides.

MOUNTAIN BIKING   There are numerous opportunities for mountain biking in the national forest, but only on roads and specified trails. A particularly popular route is **Dave's Hollow Trail,** which starts at the Bryce Canyon National Park boundary sign on Utah 63, the park entrance road, about 1 mile south of Ruby's Inn. The double-track trail goes west for about a half mile before connecting with Forest Road 090, where you turn south and ride for about three-quarters of a mile before turning right onto an easy ride through Dave's Hollow to the Dave's Hollow Forest Service Station on Forest Road 087. From here you can retrace your route for an 8-mile round-trip ride; for a longer 12-mile loop, turn right on Forest Road 087 to Utah 12 and then right again back to Utah 63 and the starting point. A third option is to turn left on Forest Road 087 and follow it to Tropic Reservoir (see "Fishing," above).

The **Casto Canyon Trail,** in Red Canyon, is an especially scenic trail open to hikers, mountain bikers, and those on horseback (see "Hiking," above).

For information on local mountain bike rentals, stop at the Red Canyon Visitor Center (see "Information & Visitor Center," above).

WINTER ACTIVITIES   Cross-country skiing and snowshoeing opportunities abound along trails and old roads in the national forest, and snowmobiling is also popular. Best Western Ruby's Inn (see "Where to Stay" in chapter 8) grooms over 30 miles (50 km) of cross-country ski trails for skating and classical skiing, and also rents equipment. Use of the trails is free; ski rentals cost $7 for a half-day and $10 for a full day.

3 Cedar Breaks National Monument

85 miles N of the main section of Zion National Park; 56 miles W of Bryce Canyon National Park

A delightful little park, Cedar Breaks is a wonderful place to spend anywhere from a few hours to several days, gazing down from the rim into the spectacular natural amphitheater, hiking the trails, and camping among the spruce and fir trees.

This natural coliseum, which reminds us of Bryce Canyon, is more than 2,000 feet deep and over 3 miles across; it's filled with stone spires, arches, and columns painted in ever-changing reds, purples, oranges, and ochers. But why "Cedar Breaks"? Well, the pioneers who came here called such badlands "breaks," and they mistook the juniper trees along the cliff bases for cedars.

JUST THE FACTS

At over 10,000 feet elevation, it's always pleasantly cool at Cedar Breaks. It actually gets downright cold at night, so bring a jacket or sweater, even if the temperature is scorching just down the road in St. George. The monument opens for its short summer season only after the snow melts, usually in late May, and closes in mid-October— unless you happen to have a snowmobile or a pair of cross-country skis or snowshoes, in which case you can visit year-round.

GETTING THERE   From Zion's south entrance, head west on Utah 9, then north on Utah 17 to I-15. Follow the interstate north to exit 57 for Cedar City, and head east on Utah 14 to Utah 148. Turn north (left), and follow Utah 148 into the monument. From the Kolob Canyons section of Zion, which is just off exit 40 of I-15, it is only 40 miles to Cedar Breaks. If you're coming from Bryce Canyon or other points east, the park is accessible from the town of Panguitch via Utah 143. If you're traveling from the north, take the Parowan exit off I-15 and head south on Utah 143. It's a steep climb from whichever direction you choose, and vehicles prone to vapor lock or loss of power on hills (such as RVs) may have some problems.

INFORMATION/VISITOR CENTER   A mile from the south entrance gate, you'll find the **visitor center,** open daily from early June to mid-October, with exhibits on the geology, flora, and fauna of Cedar Breaks. You can purchase books and maps here, and rangers can help plan your visit. For advance information, contact the Superintendent, **Cedar Breaks National Monument,** 2390 West Utah 56, Suite 11, Cedar City, UT 84720-4151 (🆓 **435/ 586-9451;** www.nps.gov/cebr).

FEES & REGULATIONS Admission costs $3 per person for all those 17 and older. Regulations are similar to those at most national parks: Leave everything as you find it. Mountain bikes are not allowed on hiking trails. Dogs, which must be leashed at all times, are prohibited on all trails, in the backcountry, and in public buildings.

HEALTH & SAFETY CONCERNS The high elevation—10,350 feet at the visitor center—is likely to cause shortness of breath and tiredness, and those with heart or respiratory conditions should consult their doctors before visiting. Avoid high, exposed areas during thunderstorms; they're often targets for lightning.

RANGER PROGRAMS During the monument's short summer season, rangers offer nightly campfire talks at the campground; talks on the area's geology at Point Supreme, a viewpoint near the visitor center, daily on the hour from 10am to 5pm; and guided hikes on Saturday and Sunday mornings. A complete schedule is posted at the visitor center and the campground.

EXPLORING CEDAR BREAKS BY CAR

The 5-mile road through Cedar Breaks National Monument offers easy access to the monument's scenic overlooks and trailheads. Allow 30 to 45 minutes to make the drive. Start at the visitor center and nearby **Point Supreme** for a panoramic view of the amphitheater. Then drive north, past the campground and picnic ground turnoff, to **Sunset View** for a closer view of the amphitheater and its colorful canyons. From each of these overlooks, you'll be able to see out across Cedar Valley, over the Antelope and Black Mountains, into the Escalante Desert.

Continue north to **Chessman Ridge Overlook,** so named because the hoodoos directly below look like massive stone chess pieces. Watch for swallows and swifts soaring among the rock formations. Then head north to **Alpine Pond,** a trailhead for a self-guided nature trail (see "Hiking," below) with an abundance of wildflowers. Finally, you'll reach **North View,** which offers your best look into the amphitheater. The view here is reminiscent of Bryce Canyon's Queen's Garden, with its stately statues frozen in time.

SPORTS & ACTIVITIES

CAMPING The 30-site campground, **Point Supreme,** just north of the visitor center, is open from June to mid-September, with sites available on a first-come, first-served basis. It's a beautiful high-mountain setting, among tall spruce and fir. Facilities include restrooms, drinking water, picnic tables, grills, and an amphitheater for the ranger's evening campfire programs. No showers or RV hookups are available. Camping fee is $10 per night. Keep in mind that even in midsummer, temperatures can drop into the 30s at night at this elevation, so bring cool-weather gear.

HIKING   There are no trails from the rim to the bottom of the amphitheater, but the monument does have two high-country trails. The fairly easy 2-mile **Alpine Pond Trail** loop leads through a woodland of bristlecone pines to a picturesque forest glade and pond surrounded by wildflowers, offering panoramic views of the amphitheater along the way. A trail guide is available at the trailhead.

A somewhat more challenging hike, the 4-mile **Spectra Point Trail** (or Ramparts Trail) follows the rim more closely than the Alpine Pond Trail, offering changing views of the colorful rock formations. It also takes you through fields of wildflowers and by bristlecone pines more than 1,500 years old. Be especially careful of your footing along the exposed cliff edges, and allow yourself some time to rest—there are lots of ups and downs along the way.

WILDLIFE WATCHING   Because of its relative remoteness, Cedar Breaks is a good place for spotting wildlife. You're likely to see mule deer grazing in the meadows along the road early and late in the day. Marmots make their dens near the rim and are often seen along the Spectra Point Trail. You'll spot ground squirrels, red squirrels, and chipmunks everywhere. Pikas, which are related to rabbits, are here too, but it's unlikely you'll see one. They're small, with short ears and stubby tails, and prefer the high, rocky slopes.

Finds A Late Summer Bonanza: The Wildflowers of Cedar Breaks

During its brief summer season, Cedar Breaks makes the most of the warmth and moisture in the air with a spectacular wildflower show. The rim comes alive in a blaze of color—truly a sight to behold. The dazzling display begins practically as soon as the snow melts and reaches its peak during late July and August. Watch for mountain bluebells, spring beauty, beard tongue, and fleabane early in the season; those beauties then make way for columbine, larkspur, Indian paintbrush, wild roses, and other varieties.

In the campground, look for Clark's nutcrackers, with their gray torsos and black-and-white wings and tails. The monument is also home to swallows, swifts, blue grouse, and golden eagles.

WINTER ACTIVITIES The monument's facilities are shut down from mid-October to late May due to the thick blanket of snow that covers it. The snow-blocked roads keep cars out, but they're perfect for snowmobilers, snowshoers, and cross-country skiers, who usually come over from nearby Brian Head ski area. Snowshoers and cross country skiers have a variety of options, but snowmobiles are restricted to the main 5-mile road through the monument, which is groomed and marked.

4 Grand Staircase–Escalante National Monument

Covering some 1.9 million acres, this vast area of red-orange canyons, mesas, plateaus, and river valleys became a national monument on September 18, 1996. Known for its stark, rugged beauty, it contains a unique combination of geological, biological, paleontological, archaeological, and historical resources.

In announcing the creation of the monument, President Bill Clinton proclaimed, "This high, rugged, and remote region was the last place in the continental United States to be mapped; even today, this unspoiled natural area remains a frontier, a quality that greatly enhances the monument's value for scientific study." While hailed by environmentalists, the president's action was not popular in Utah, largely because the area contains a great deal of coal and other valuable resources. Utah Senator Orrin Hatch denounced Clinton's decree, calling it "the mother of all land-grabs."

Under the jurisdiction of the Bureau of Land Management, the monument is expected to remain open for grazing and possible oil and gas drilling under existing leases (no new leases will be issued), as well as hunting, fishing, hiking, camping, and other recreation.

Unlike most other national monuments, almost all of this vast area is undeveloped—there are few all-weather roads, only one maintained hiking trail, and two developed campgrounds. But the adventurous will find miles upon miles of dirt roads and practically unlimited opportunities for hiking, horseback riding, mountain biking on existing dirt roads, and camping.

The national monument can be divided into three distinct sections: the **Grand Staircase** of sandstone cliffs, which includes five life zones from Sonoran Desert to coniferous forests, in the southwest; the **Kaiparowits Plateau,** a vast, wild region of rugged mesas

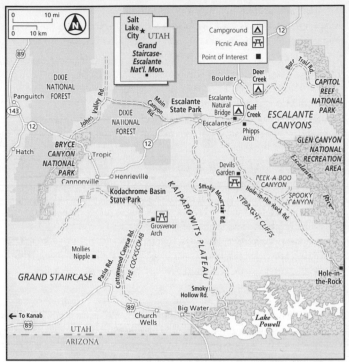

and steep canyons in the center; and the **Escalante River Canyons** section, along the northern edge of the monument, a delightfully scenic area containing miles of interconnecting river canyons.

JUST THE FACTS

Over such a vast area, weather conditions vary greatly, but it's safe to say that summers are hot. As with most parts of southern Utah, spring and fall are the best times to visit.

GETTING THERE The national monument takes in a large section of southern Utah—covering an area almost as big as the states of Delaware and Rhode Island combined—with Bryce Canyon National Park to the west, Capitol Reef National Park on its northeast edge, and Glen Canyon National Recreation Area along the east and part of the south sides.

Access is via Utah 12 along the monument's northern boundary, from Kodachrome Basin State Park and the communities of

Escalante and Boulder; and via U.S. 89 to the southwestern section of the monument, east of the town of Kanab, which is about 80 miles south of Bryce Canyon.

INFORMATION & VISITOR CENTERS Stop at the **Escalante Interagency Office,** on the west side of Escalante at 755 W. Main St. (Utah 12), (© **435/826-5499**); or contact the **Bureau of Land Management/Monument Office,** 318 N. 100 East St., Kanab, UT 84741 (© **435/644-2672;** www.ut.blm.gov/ monument). These offices offer maps and handouts on a variety of activities.

FEES, REGULATIONS, & SAFETY There is no charge to enter the monument; those planning overnight trips into the backcountry should obtain free permits at either of the offices listed above. Regulations are similar to those on other public lands, but damaging or disturbing archaeological and historic sites in any way is particularly forbidden.

Water is the main safety concern here. This is generally very dry country, so carry plenty of drinking water. However, thunderstorms can turn the monument's dirt roads into impassable mud bogs in minutes, stranding motorists; and potentially fatal flash floods through narrow canyons can catch hikers by surprise. Anyone planning trips into the monument should check first with one of the offices listed above on current and anticipated weather and travel conditions, and you should be alert to changing conditions while exploring the monument.

SPORTS & ACTIVITIES

CAMPING There are two designated campgrounds in the monument. **Calf Creek Campground,** in the Calf Creek Recreation Area about 15 miles northeast of the town of Escalante via Utah 12, has 13 sites and a picnic area. Open year-round, the tree-shaded campground is situated in a scenic, steep canyon along Calf Creek, surrounded by high rock walls. Facilities include a volleyball court, an interpretive hiking trail (see "Hiking, Mountain Biking & Horseback Riding," below), flush toilets, and drinking water, but no showers, RV hookups, RV dump station, or trash removal. In summer, the campground is often full by 10am. November through March, water is turned off and only vault toilets are available. Vehicles must ford a shallow creek, and the campground is not recommended for vehicles over 25 feet long. Campsites cost $7 per night; day use is $2 per vehicle.

Impressions

On this remarkable site, God's handiwork is everywhere.
—President Bill Clinton, September 18, 1996

The national monument's other designated campground is **Deer Creek,** located 6 miles east of the town of Boulder along the scenic Burr Trail Road. Camping at the four primitive sites here costs $4; no drinking water or other facilities are available.

Backcountry camping is permitted in most areas of the monument with a free permit, available at the Interagency Office in Escalante and BLM office in Kanab (see above).

HIKING, MOUNTAIN BIKING & HORSEBACK RIDING Located about 15 miles northeast of Escalante via Utah 12, the **Calf Creek Recreation Area** has a campground (see "Camping," above), and a picnic area with fire grates and tables, trees, drinking water, and flush toilets. The best part of the recreation area, though, is the moderately strenuous 5½-mile round-trip hike to **Lower Calf Creek Falls.** A sandy trail leads along Calf Creek, past beaver ponds and wetlands, to a beautiful waterfall, cascading 126 feet down a rock wall into a tree-shaded pool. You can pick up an interpretive brochure at the trailhead.

Although **Calf Creek Trail** is the monument's only officially marked and maintained trail, numerous unmarked cross-country routes are ideal for hiking, mountain biking (on existing dirt roads only), and horseback riding. We strongly recommend that hikers stop at the Interagency Office in Escalante or the BLM office in Kanab to get recommendations on hiking routes and to purchase topographic maps. Hikers need to remember that this is wild country and can be hazardous. Rangers recommend carrying at least 1 gallon of water per person per day, and say that all water from streams should be treated before drinking. The potential for flooding is high, and hikers should check with the BLM before attempting to hike through the monument's narrow slot canyons. Other hazards include poisonous snakes, scorpions and poison ivy. Slickrock, as the name suggests, is slippery, so hikers should wear sturdy hiking boots with traction soles.

Among popular and relatively easy-to-follow hiking routes is the footpath to **Escalante Natural Bridge;** it repeatedly crosses the river, so be prepared to get wet up to your knees. The easy 2-mile (one-way) hike begins at a parking area at the bridge that crosses the

Escalante River near Calf Creek Recreation Area, 15 miles northeast of the town of Escalante. From the parking area, hike upstream to Escalante Natural Bridge, on the south side of the river. The bridge is 130 feet high and spans 100 feet.

Also starting at the Utah 12 bridge parking area is a hike downstream to **Phipps Wash.** Mostly moderate, this hike goes about 1½ miles to the mouth of Phipps Wash, which enters the river from the west. You'll find Maverick Natural Bridge in a north side drainage of Phipps Wash, and climbing up the drainage on the south side leads to Phipps Arch.

Hiking the national monument's **slot canyons** is very popular, but we can't overemphasize the importance of checking on flood potentials before starting out. A sudden rainstorm, even one that's miles away, can cause a flash flood through a narrow canyon, trapping hikers.

One challenging and very strenuous slot-canyon hike is through **Peek-a-boo** and **Spooky canyons,** which are accessible from the Hole-in-the-Rock Scenic Backway (see "Sightseeing & Four-wheeling," below). Stop at the Escalante Interagency Office for precise directions.

SIGHTSEEING & FOUR-WHEELING   Since this is one of America's least-developed sections of public land, it offers a wonderful opportunity for exploration by the adventurous. Be aware, though, that the dirt roads inside the monument turn muddy—and impassable—when it rains.

One particularly popular road is the **Hole-in-the-Rock Scenic Backway,** which is partly in the national monument and partly in the adjacent Glen Canyon National Recreation Area. Like most roads in the monument, this should be attempted in dry weather only. Starting about 5 miles northeast of Escalante off Utah 12, this clearly marked dirt road travels 57 miles (one-way) to the Hole-in-the-Rock, where Mormon settlers, in 1880, cut a passage through solid rock to get their wagons down a 1,200-foot cliff to the canyon floor and Colorado River below.

Impressions

These cliffs are bold escarpments hundreds and thousands of feet in altitude—grand steps by which the region is terraced.

—Maj. John Wesley Powell (1880)

About 12 miles in, the road passes by the sign to **Devil's Rock Garden,** an area of classic red rock formations and arches, where you'll also find a picnic area (about a mile off the main road). The road continues across a plateau of typical desert terrain, ending at a spectacular scenic overlook of Lake Powell. The first 35 miles of the scenic byway are relatively easy (in dry weather) in a standard passenger car; it then gets a bit steeper and sandier, and the last 6 miles of the road require a high clearance 4×4 vehicle. Allow about 6 hours round-trip, and make sure you have plenty of fuel and water.

Another recommended drive in the national monument is the **Cottonwood Canyon Road,** which runs from Kodachrome Basin State Park south to U.S. 89, along the monument's southern edge, a distance of about 46 miles. The road is sandy and narrow, but usually passable for passenger cars in dry weather. It mostly follows Cottonwood Wash, with good views of red rock formations and distant panoramas from hilltops. About 10 miles east of Kodachrome Basin State Park, you'll find a short side road to **Grosvenor Arch.** This magnificent stone arch, with an opening 99 feet wide, was named for National Geographic Society founder and editor Gilbert H. Grosvenor. Incidentally, a professional photographer friend of ours complained bitterly about the power lines that parallel the road, making scenic photography difficult. However, the BLM tells us that the road wouldn't exist at all if it weren't for those power lines.

WILDLIFE VIEWING & BIRD-WATCHING   This isolated and rugged terrain makes a good habitat for a number of species, including desert bighorn sheep and mountain lions. More than 200 species of birds have been seen, including bald eagles, golden eagles, Swainson's hawks, and peregrine falcons. The best areas for seeing wildlife are along the Escalante and Paria rivers and Johnson Creek.

5 Kodachrome Basin State Park

About 22 miles E of the entrance to Bryce Canyon National Park

Kodachrome Basin lives up to its name; its wonderful scenery practically cries out to be captured on film (regardless of brand or type). Named by the National Geographic Society in 1949, the park is chock-full of tall stone "chimneys" and pink-and-white sandstone cliffs, all set among the contrasting greens of sagebrush and piñon and juniper trees. It also abuts and makes a good base for exploring Grand Staircase–Escalante National Monument (see above).

JUST THE FACTS

Because temperatures get a bit warm here in summer—the park is at 5,800 feet elevation—the best times to visit, especially for hikers, are May, September, and October, when there are also fewer people.

GETTING THERE   From Bryce Canyon National Park, go 3 miles north to the junction of Utah 63 and Utah 12, go east (right) on Utah 12 for about 12 miles to Cannonville, turn south onto the park's access road (there's a sign), and go about 7 miles to the park entrance.

INFORMATION, FEES & REGULATIONS   Contact the **park office** at P.O. Box 238, Cannonville, UT 84718 (✆ **435/ 679-8562**). Day use costs $4 per vehicle or $2 per person entering by foot, bicycle, or motorcycle. Dogs are permitted in the park and on trails, but must be kept on leashes no more than 6 feet long.

SPORTS & ACTIVITIES

CAMPING   The park's attractive 24-site campground is set among stone chimneys and scattered piñon and juniper trees. It has flush toilets, showers, drinking water, picnic tables, barbecue grills, and an RV dump station, but no RV hookups. Campsites cost $13 per night. Call ✆ **800/322-3770** for reservations; a $6.25 nonrefundable reservation fee will be charged.

HIKING   Kodachrome Basin offers several hiking possibilities. Starting just south of the campground, the **Panorama Trail** is only moderately difficult. At first, it follows an old, relatively flat wagon route, then climbs to offer views of the park's rock formations before reaching the well-named Panorama Point. Along the way are several possible side trips, including a short walk to the **Hat Shop,** so named because the formations resemble broad-brimmed hats, and **White Buffalo Loop,** where you'll see a formation that looks like— guess what?—a white buffalo. The optional **Big Bear Geyser Trail** is a bit more difficult, winding past Big Bear and Mama Bear before returning to Panorama Trail. Allow 2 to 3 hours for the Panorama Trail and an extra hour for Big Bear Geyser Trail.

Fans of arches will want to drive the dirt road to the trailhead for the half-mile round-trip hike to **Shakespeare Arch,** discovered by park manager Tom Shakespeare. This trail also provides views of a large chimney-rock formation.

HORSEBACK RIDING & STAGECOACH RIDES   Located in the park, **Trail Head Station** (✆ **435/679-8536** or 435/679-8787;

www.brycecanyoninn.com) offers horseback and stagecoach rides April through October. Horseback rides start at $15 per hour and 1-hour stagecoach rides cost $12. The company also rents six cabins (full bath, refrigerator, and an outside barbecue grill for cooking) for $65 per night for up to four people; and operates a small store with camping supplies, food items, and the like.

WILDLIFE WATCHING   Jackrabbits and chukar partridges are probably the most commonly seen wildlife in the park. You'll also hear the piñon jay and might see an occasional coyote or rattlesnake.

6 Coral Pink Sand Dunes State Park

About 45 miles SE of Zion National Park

Long a favorite of dune-buggy enthusiasts, Coral Pink Sand Dunes has recently been attracting an increasing number of campers, hikers, photographers, and all-around nature lovers as well. While big boys—and occasionally big girls—play with their expensive motorized toys, others hike; hunt for wildflowers, scorpions, and lizards; or just sit and wiggle their toes in the smooth, cool sand. The colors are especially rich at sunrise and sunset. Early-morning visitors will find the tracks of yesterday's dune buggies gone, replaced by the tracks of lizards, kangaroo rats, snakes, and the rest of the park's animal kingdom, who venture out in the coolness of night once all the people have departed.

JUST THE FACTS

At about 5,800 feet elevation, the park gets warm in summer, with temperatures easily reaching the mid 90s, and winters are usually relatively mild, although snow and bitter cold temperatures are not unheard of. Our choice for a visit is May, June, September, or October, when it's delightfully cool at night but warm enough during the day to enjoy burying your toes in the cooling sand. And there are also fewer people there at those times.

GETTING THERE   From Zion National Park, take Utah 9 east to U.S. 89, turn right (south) and continue to the park entrance road. From downtown Kanab, go about 8 miles north on U.S. 89, then southwest (left) on Hancock Road for about 12 miles to get to the park.

INFORMATION & VISITOR CENTER   For copies of the park brochure and off-highway-vehicle regulations, contact the **park office** at P.O. Box 95, Kanab, UT 84741-0095 (© **435/648-2800**).

At the **park entry station,** you'll see a small display area with sand from around the world, fossils of the area, and live scorpions, lizards, and tadpoles.

FEES & REGULATIONS   The day-use fee is $4 per vehicle, $2 per person on foot or bike. The standard state park regulations apply, with the addition of a few extra rules due to the park's popularity with off-road-vehicle users. Quiet hours last from 10pm to 9am. The dunes are open to motor vehicles between 9am and 10pm and to hikers at any time. Vehicles going onto the dunes must have safety flags, available at the entry station; while on the dunes, they must stay at least 10 feet from vegetation and at least 100 feet from hikers. Dogs are permitted on the dunes but must be leashed.

RANGER PROGRAMS   Regularly scheduled ranger talks explain the geology, plants, and animals of the dunes. For a real thrill, take a guided evening **Scorpion Walk** 🐾🐾, using a black light to find luminescent scorpions that make the park their home. You'll definitely want to wear shoes for this activity! Call to find out if there's one scheduled during your visit.

OUTDOOR PURSUITS

CAMPING   The spacious and mostly shady 22-site campground, open year-round, offers hot showers, modern restrooms, and an RV dump station, but no hookups. Camping costs $13. Call ✆ **800/ 322-3770** for reservations, with a $6.25 non-refundable reservation fee.

HIKING   The best time for hiking the dunes is early morning, for several reasons: It's cooler, the lighting at and just after sunrise produces beautiful shadows and colors, and there are no noisy dune buggies until after 9am. Sunset is also very pretty, but you'll be sharing the dunes with off-road vehicles. Keep in mind that hiking through fine sand can be very tiring, especially for those who go barefoot. A self-guided half-mile loop nature trail has numbered signs through some of the dunes; allow a half hour.

Several other hikes of various lengths are possible within and just outside the park, but because there are few signs—and because landmarks change with the shifting sands—it's best to check with park rangers before setting out. Those spending more than a few hours in the dunes will discover that even their own tracks disappear in the wind, leaving few clues to the route back to park headquarters.

OFF-ROADING   This giant 1,000-acre sandbox offers plenty of space for **off-road-vehicle enthusiasts.** Because the sand here is quite fine, extra-wide flotation tires are needed, and lightweight dune buggies are usually the vehicle of choice. Adjacent to the park on Bureau of Land Management property, you'll find hundreds of miles of trails and roads for off-highway vehicles.

7 Escalante State Park

48 miles E of Bryce Canyon National Park

Large chunks of colorful petrified wood decorate this unique park, which offers hiking, fishing, boating, camping, and panoramic vistas of the surrounding countryside. There's wildlife to watch, trails to hike, and a 30-acre reservoir for boating, fishing, and somewhat chilly swimming.

JUST THE FACTS

The park is open all year, but spring through fall are the best times to visit. Hikers should be prepared for hot summer temperatures and carry plenty of water, though.

GETTING THERE   The park is 48 miles from Bryce Canyon. It's located about 2 miles southwest of Escalante on Utah 12, at Wide Hollow Road.

INFORMATION & VISITOR CENTER   Contact **Escalante State Park,** P.O. Box 350, Escalante, UT 84726-0350 (© **435/ 826-4466**). The **visitor center** has displays of petrified wood, dinosaur bones, and fossils, plus an exhibit explaining how petrified wood is formed.

FEES & REGULATIONS   Entry costs $4 per vehicle and $2 for pedestrians or bicyclists for day use. As at most parks, regulations are generally based on common sense and courtesy: Don't damage anything, drive slowly on park roads, and observe quiet hours between 10pm and 7am. In addition, you're asked to resist the temptation to carry off samples of petrified wood. Pets are welcome, even on trails, but must be on leashes no more than 6 feet long.

SPORTS & ACTIVITIES

CAMPING   The 22-unit **campground,** within easy walking distance of the park's hiking trails and reservoir, is open year-round. Facilities include hot showers, modern restrooms, and drinking water, but no RV hookups. Camping costs $13 per night. Call

Rock or Wood—What Is This Stuff?

It looks like a weathered, multicolored tree limb, shining and sparkling in the light—but it's heavy, hard, and solid as a rock. Just what is this stuff? It's petrified wood.

Back in the old days—some 135 to 155 million years ago—southern Utah was not at all the way it is today. It was closer to the equator than it is now, which made it a wet, hot land, with lots of ferns, palm trees, and conifers that provided lunch for the neighborhood dinosaurs.

Occasionally, floods would uproot trees, dumping them in flood plains and along sandbars, then burying them with mud and silt. If this happened quickly, the layers of mud and silt would cut off the oxygen supply, halting the process of decomposition—effectively preserving the tree trunks intact.

Later, volcanic ash covered the area, and groundwater rich in silicon dioxide and other chemicals and minerals made its way down to the ancient trees. With the silicon dioxide acting as a glue, the cells of the wood mineralized. Other waterborne minerals produced the colors: Iron painted the tree trunks in reds, browns, and yellows; manganese produced purples and blues.

Sometime afterward, uplifts from within the earth, along with various forms of erosion, brought the now-petrified wood to the surface (in places like Escalante State Park and the Grand Staircase–Escalante National Monument), breaking it into the shapes we see today—a mere hundred million years or so after the trees were first uprooted.

☎ 800/322-3770 for reservations; a $6.25 nonrefundable fee will be charged.

FISHING & BOATING   Wide Hollow Reservoir, located partially inside the park, has a boat ramp (sorry, no rentals are available) and is a popular fishing hole for rainbow trout and bluegill, plus ice-fishing in winter.

HIKING   The 1-mile **Petrified Forest Trail** 🐾 is a moderately strenuous hike among colorful rocks, through a forest of stunted juniper and piñon pine, past a painted desert, to a field of colorful petrified wood. The hike also offers panoramic vistas of the town of Escalante and surrounding stair-step plateaus. A free brochure is available at the visitor center. Allow about 45 minutes. An optional three-quarter-mile loop off the main trail leads through more petrified wood, but is considerably steeper than the main trail.

WILDLIFE WATCHING   This is one of the best spots in the region to see wildlife. The reservoir is home to ducks, geese, and coots. Chukar partridges wander throughout the park, and you're also likely to see eagles, hawks, lizards, ground squirrels, and both cottontails and jackrabbits. Binoculars are helpful.

8 Snow Canyon State Park

11 miles NW of St. George; about 60 miles W of Zion National Park

Among Utah's most scenic state parks, **Snow Canyon** 🏵🏵 offers an abundance of opportunities for photography and hiking. The park is surrounded by rock cliffs and walls of Navajo sandstone in every shade of red imaginable, layered with white and black from ancient lava flows. Hike the trails and discover shifting sand dunes, mysterious lava caves, colorful desert plants, and a variety of rock formations. You'll also encounter an attractive cactus garden, whose plants are described in a brochure, and several ancient petroglyphs (ask park rangers for directions). By the way, don't come here looking for snow—Snow Canyon was named for pioneers Lorenzo and Erastus Snow, who found it.

JUST THE FACTS

Because the summers here are hot—well over 100°F—the best time to visit is any other time. Winters are mild, but nights can be chilly. Spring and fall are usually perfect weatherwise, and are therefore the busiest.

GETTING THERE   From Zion National Park, follow Utah 9 to I-15, exit 16; head south to St. George (exit 8); take Utah 18 northwest to the park's entrance road.

INFORMATION, FEES & REGULATIONS   For a copy of the park's brochure, contact **Snow Canyon State Park Headquarters,** P.O. Box 140, Santa Clara, UT 84765-0140 (✆ **435/628-2255**). Day-use fee is $4 per vehicle, or $2 per person on foot, bike, or motorcycle. As in most state parks, dogs are welcome, including on trails, but must be leashed.

SPORTS & ACTIVITIES

CAMPING The 36-site campground is one of the best in the state. One section has rather closely spaced sites with electric hookups; those not needing electricity can set up camp in delightful little side canyons, surrounded by colorful red rocks and Utah juniper. The views are spectacular no matter where you choose to set up. Facilities include hot showers, modern restrooms, and an RV dump station. Campsites with electricity cost $15, while those without are $13. Reservations (with a $6.25 nonrefundable reservation fee) are recommended February through May and September through November; call ✆ **800/322-3770.**

HIKING The best way to see Snow Canyon is on foot. Several short trails make for easy full- or half-day hikes. The **Hidden Piñon Trail** is a 1½-mile round-trip self-guided nature trail that wanders among lava rocks, through several canyons, and onto rocky flatlands, offering panoramic views of the surrounding mountains. The trail begins across the highway from the campground; you can pick up a brochure at the park office/entrance station. The walk is fairly easy, but allow at least an hour. Keep an eye out for Mormon tea, cliffrose, prickly pear cactus, and banana yucca.

An easy three-quarter-mile one-way trail leads to **Johnson Arch.** It begins just south of the campground, passes by the popular rock-climbing wall (see below), some low sand dunes, and then a small canyon with a view of Johnson Arch (named after pioneer wife Maude Johnson) high above.

Also popular is the **Lava Caves Trail,** a 1½-mile round-trip that starts just north of the campground. The caves are about a half mile along the trail, but watch carefully—it's easy to miss them. The caves were formed from liquid lava, and American Indian tribes have at times occupied the large rooms. Another quarter mile past the caves is the **West Canyon Overlook,** with a breathtaking view into West Canyon.

Several longer and steeper trails lead to spectacular views of the canyons and distant vistas; check with park rangers for details.

MOUNTAIN BIKING Although bicycling is not allowed on park trails, West Canyon Road is open to mountain biking. The 7-mile (round-trip) road lies just west of the park; ask park rangers for directions.

ROCK CLIMBING Climbers love the tall wall of rock on the east side of the road just south of the campground, but it has become so popular that the park has issued a moratorium on bolting. Check with the park office for information.

WILDLIFE WATCHING   You're likely to see cottontail rabbits, ground squirrels, and songbirds; luckier visitors may also spot desert mule deer, bobcats, coyote, kit foxes, eagles, and owls. Although it's unlikely, you may see a desert tortoise (a federally listed threatened species) or Gila monster. Snow Canyon is also home to some rattlesnakes, which you'll want to avoid.

A Nature Guide to Zion & Bryce Canyon National Parks

Magnificently diverse, Zion and Bryce Canyon National Parks contain burning deserts, lush woodlands with shimmering ponds, barren, windswept ledges of solid rock, and deep forests of pine and fir. These habitats, with their variety of terrain and climates, support a wide array of plants and animals, in a diversity that is primarily the result of elevation and availability of water. Zion, ranging from 3,666 feet to 8,726 feet above sea level, has a larger variety of plants and animals than cooler and higher Bryce Canyon, with elevations from 6,620 feet to 9,115 feet.

1 Zion & Bryce Canyon National Parks Today

While much of southern Utah is barren and sometimes drab desert, Zion and Bryce Canyon are most certainly much more (that is, of course, why they were designated national parks in the first place). Those with the time and inclination to explore these parks will discover hundreds of microclimates—little worlds of their own that create unique habitats that often seem out of place in this generally arid country.

In Zion, you can see several of these microclimates along the **Riverside Walk**—there's a desert swamp where you might spot a leopard frog or two, and lush, hanging gardens on the walls as you enter **the Narrows.** You'll also find hanging gardens at **Zion's Weeping Rock,** where there is a good example of *spring lines*—when water seeping through a porous rock is diverted to the surface by a layer of much harder rock.

At Bryce Canyon you'll discover a moist world in the aptly named **Mossy Cave,** which is fed by a natural spring. Walking down the **Queen's Garden Trail,** you'll notice that vegetation on the north facing slopes and in narrow gullies—Douglas fir and ponderosa pines—is far different than the piñon and juniper in the sunnier areas. And there is a much cooler and wetter climate at the higher elevations in the southern section of the park—such as along the **Bristlecone Loop** and **Riggs Spring Loop** trails.

Bryce Canyon at first seems easy to understand—it's the hoodoos—but look a bit closer and you soon come to realize that in addition to its delightful rock formations, Bryce Canyon has serene woodlands of pine where deer graze in open meadows, and dense forests of spruce and fir, where you also find the world's oldest living things—bristlecone pines. Of course, there are also the lowlands, below the rim. This is definitely a desert, yet anything but drab, with its colorful and whimsical hoodoos.

Zion has a more complicated environment. It has stupendous rock formations—even a few hoodoos of its own—but it also has the unique Narrows, a canyon carved by the Virgin River with fascinating microclimates and habitats that support plants and animals not seen elsewhere in the park. These include the rare Zion snail, found nowhere else in the world. In some ways, Zion seems to have more extremes than Bryce Canyon, ranging from delightful little pools surrounded by delicate ferns and wildflowers, to rocky, windswept ridges, where only the most determined and rugged plants and animals can survive.

The best way to explore these parks and get to know them intimately is to get away from the viewpoints and take to the trails, leaving behind the throngs, who seem to be glued to the officially designated scenic lookouts. Remember, though, that southern Utah is hot in the summer, and these parks—particularly lower-elevation Zion and some of the trails below the rim at Bryce Canyon—can be scorching desert, so be prepared as you hit the trail.

On the other hand, it is also possible to get a close-up view of nature without exerting a lot of effort. Plants and rocks are everywhere, and a variety of animals can be seen throughout both parks. To see wildlife, simply go to a quiet place—even a park campground early in the morning—and wait. Sit at the edge of a meadow or take a slow walk down almost any park path or trail—the key here is to get away from people, and especially the noise they make, and take the time to watch, wait, and listen. Nature surrounds you at both Bryce Canyon and Zion National Parks, but it doesn't necessarily advertise itself; with just a bit of patience, it can be coaxed out of hiding.

2 The Landscape

There are many reasons to visit Zion and Bryce Canyon National Parks, but what you'll find in almost all sections of both parks—and probably what you came to experience—are their intricately sculpted and often beautifully colored rocks, from majestic, towering formations like the Great White Throne at Zion, to the delicately carved and whimsical hoodoos at Bryce Canyon. For these we can thank the geologic processes of uplifting and erosion.

The parks are located on the northwestern edge of the Colorado Plateau, a 130,000-square-mile region that covers the Four Corners area and encompasses about half of Utah, most of northern Arizona (including the Grand Canyon), much of western Colorado, and the northwest corner of New Mexico. Named for the Colorado River, which is responsible for carving many of the area's scenic canyons, the Colorado Plateau began as the result of uplifting 10 to 15 million years ago. In simple terms, the large, flat beds of sedimentary rock created from different materials—or different combinations of the same materials—resulted in layers of varying densities. Forces within the earth pushed some of these sections of sediment up into the air. This is especially noticeable in places such as Zion and Bryce Canyon. Here, uplifts along geologic fault lines created high plateaus with large chunks of rock, where you can see the stripes of the different layers.

When wind and water began their inevitable erosion, layers of softer rock, such as sandstone and limestone, wore down faster than the harder layers of mudstone and shale. This created intricate and sometimes bizarre shapes. This erosion, as well as the shifting and breaking of rock, carved the sculptures of Zion and Bryce Canyon. The process almost always involves water and gravity, although wind and temperature, primarily freezing and thawing, play an important role as well.

The formation called **Thor's Hammer** in Bryce Canyon, for example, owes its hammerlike shape to a variety of rock densities—the hammer section on top is harder and more resistant to erosion than the softer handle section below. Eventually, the handle will crumble and the hammerhead will come crashing to the ground.

Although there are also hoodoos similar to Thor's Hammer in Zion—mostly on the park's east side—many of Zion's rock formations appear more massive and rugged, and in some ways very different. But here, too, the rocks have simply been carved by the forces of nature, primarily water, as can be seen clearly when looking up from the bottom of **the Narrows.** This incredibly slim

How Nature Paints the Parks

The shapes are fantastic—towering monoliths, massive mesas of stone, delicate spires, intricately carved sculptures, and squat little toadstools—but what first catches our eyes are the delightful colors. What seems like an infinite variety of hues elevates these parks from geologic wonders to exquisite works of art. But where do the colors come from? What dynamic forces have meticulously painted these stone sculptures so perfectly?

The answer, simply and unpoetically put, is rust. Most of the rocks at Zion and Bryce Canyon are colored by iron, or hematite (iron oxide), either contained in the original stone or carried into the rocks by groundwater. Although iron most often creates red and pink hues, frequently seen in Zion's towering sandstone faces and Bryce Canyon's spectacular amphitheaters, it can also result in blacks, browns, yellows, and even greens. Sometimes the iron seeps into the rock, coloring it through, but it can also stain just the surface, often in vertical streaks.

Rocks are also colored by the bacteria that live on their surfaces. These bacteria ingest dust and expel iron, manganese, and other minerals, which then stick to the rock, producing a shiny black, brown, or reddish surface called desert varnish. Last, but certainly not least, is the work of water, which deposits salt as it evaporates, creating white streaks.

canyon—1,000 feet high but less than 30 feet wide in some places—was meticulously carved through Navajo sandstone by the North Fork of the Virgin River.

The most important of Zion's nine rock layers—at least as concerns its ability to create imposing rock formations—is **Navajo sandstone,** the thickest rock layer in the park, at up to 2,200 feet. The sandstone layer was created some 200 million years ago, during the Jurassic period, when most of North America was hot and dry. Movements in the earth's crust enabled a shallow sea to form over windblown sand dunes. Then minerals, including lime from the shells of sea creatures, eventually glued sand particles together to form sandstone. Later, crust movements caused the land to uplift, draining away the sea, but leaving rivers that gradually carved the relatively soft sandstone into the spectacular shapes we see today.

By comparison, Bryce Canyon is a mere babe. Its rocks were formed some 64 million years ago, created from sediments that were left behind as ancient lakes and rivers dried up, and, as at neighboring Zion, were then uplifted and exposed to the ravages of nature. Much of Bryce Canyon's rock is **limestone,** relatively soft and crumbly, which was easily eroded into the park's numerous intricate hoodoos. And these processes continue today. Even to the naked eye, it's possible to see the changes that weathering has produced on Bryce Canyon's famous **Queen Victoria** hoodoo in only the past 25 years.

3 The Flora

Great variations in elevation and the availability of water have resulted in numerous microclimates throughout these two parks. In one section, you could see desert grasses, sagebrush, and a few cacti; while in another not far away, there might be a woods of deep green where maidenhair ferns and cottonwood trees thrive. Zion National Park boasts almost 800 native species of plant life—considered the richest diversity of plants in Utah—while at Bryce Canyon the number is closer to 400. In the lower elevations, particularly in the hot, dry desert areas of Zion, you'll find cactus, mesquite, and yucca. As elevation increases, juniper and piñon are added, and eventually, in the high mountains of Bryce Canyon, you encounter a deep forest of fir and spruce, with stands of quaking aspen that turn a magnificent bright yellow each fall.

While exploring Zion, be sure to watch for spring lines and their lush hanging gardens, which you'll see clinging to the sides of cliffs. Because sandstone is porous, water can percolate down through it until a harder layer of rock stops it. At that point the water simply changes direction, moving horizontally to the rock face, where it oozes out, forming the spring line that provides life-giving nutrients to whatever seeds the wind delivers.

TREES
ASPEN The most widely distributed tree in North America, growing from Alaska to southern Arizona, **quaking aspen** are found here above 7,500 feet elevation, mostly above the rim and in the mountains at the southern end of Bryce Canyon, and along the cliffs and plateaus at Zion. Named "quaking" for the trembling movement of the leaves at the slightest wind, aspens have white bark and almost heart-shaped green leaves that usually turn a striking yellow or gold

in the fall. Deer and elk eat the twigs and leaves, while rabbits and other small mammals eat the leaves, buds, and bark.

BRISTLECONE PINE   The oldest known trees—some have lived more than 4,600 years—bristlecones nearly 2,000 years old can be found at Bryce Canyon, usually along exposed, rocky slopes above 7,500 feet of elevation. Bristlecones are recognized by their very short, dark-green needles that grow all around the branch, often tightly packed, and dark-brown, cylindrical cones. The trees commonly have a gnarled, weathered appearance, due at least in part to their age and choice of environment.

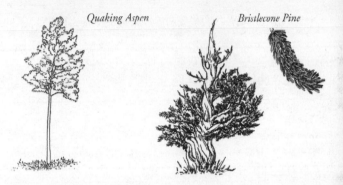

Quaking Aspen   *Bristlecone Pine*

COTTONWOOD   A member of the willow family, cottonwoods like lots of water and are usually found along streams or other permanent water sources. The **narrowleaf cottonwood,** found along water courses in Bryce Canyon, has skinny green willowlike leaves that turn dull yellow in the fall, while the **Fremont cottonwood,** found in almost all moist areas of Zion, has large, triangular-shaped, shiny yellow-green leaves that turn bright yellow in fall.

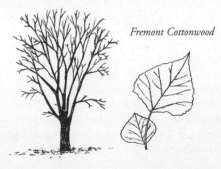

Fremont Cottonwood

DOUGLAS FIR   This large evergreen—some can grow as tall as 200 feet—has medium-sized, blue-green needles and fairly large cones. Birds and various mammals eat the seeds, while deer eat the foliage. It is found at most elevations in the canyons and on the plateaus at Zion National Park (there are good stands on the Kolob Terrace). At Bryce Canyon, you'll find Douglas fir primarily above 7,500 feet of elevation, especially in the southern part of the park.

Douglas Fir   *Juniper*

JUNIPER   Two types of juniper—**Rocky Mountain** and **Utah**— grow in the parks, most often in canyons and on rocky slopes. Utah juniper are usually seen at the lower and drier elevations—below the rim at Bryce Canyon—while Rocky Mountain juniper will grow throughout the parks up to 8,500 feet. The Utah juniper has a short trunk and low, spreading branches, with closely spaced, yellow-green needles; the Rocky Mountain juniper is often taller, sometimes reaching 50 feet, with slender branches and short, gray-green needles. Both have berrylike cones that are a popular food for birds and other wildlife. The Utah juniper's "berries" are a dull blue, while the "berries" of the Rocky Mountain juniper are bright blue with a white coating.

PIÑON PINE   Common throughout the southern Rocky Mountains between 5,000 and 7,000 feet of elevation, piñons are found at both parks, although mostly below the rim at Bryce Canyon. They are usually fairly small, somewhat gnarled, with rough bark and light green needles up to an inch and a half long that usually grow in bundles of two. The small, egg-shaped cones produce edible seeds, often called nuts, which are a popular food for both humans and wildlife. The piñon jay takes its name from the tree and its tasty seeds.

Piñon Pine

PONDEROSA PINE   This large, impressive tree, which is found in both parks, is easily recognized by its long needles—up to 10 inches—that usually grow in bundles of three. Adult trees have orange-tinted bark that has a fragrance similar to vanilla, and large, reddish-brown cones that are round or egg-shaped. At Zion, look for the ponderosa pine along cliffs and high plateaus; it is found at Bryce Canyon on sunny slopes above and along the rim, in the campgrounds, and around Bryce Canyon Lodge.

Ponderosa Pine

SHRUBS & FERNS
MAIDENHAIR FERN   A surprise in southern Utah's generally arid terrain, this moisture-loving fern, known for its delicate, lacy fronds and thin black stems, thrives in select areas of Zion National Park, near sources of water such as the Emerald Pools, and in hanging gardens, including those at Weeping Rock.

SAGEBRUSH Covering much of the American West, various types of sagebrush are found throughout Zion and Bryce Canyon. A shrub that normally grows in alkaline soil in arid areas, it can reach several feet tall if it gets sufficient water. A common food for deer and other animals, sagebrush has a fresh, pungent scent—strongest when it's wet—that is similar to the spice sage. It has tiny, gray-green leaves and sprouts small, white flowers in the fall. Three varieties grow at Bryce Canyon: **big, black,** and **fringed;** while big and **old man** grow at Zion.

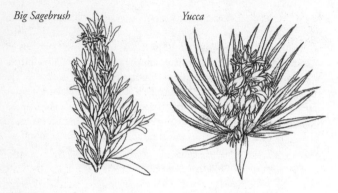

Big Sagebrush

Yucca

YUCCA Not a cactus as many think, but a shrub, yuccas grow in dry, rocky areas of both parks. One of the prettiest plants of the Southwest—absolutely stunning when it's in bloom—the yucca was extremely important to early American Indians, who made baskets and sandals from its strong leaves, ate its fruits and flowers, and turned its roots into a shampoo. The plant has long, extremely tough green leaves, which have sharp spines on their leaf tips that can be quite painful to the touch. In spring or early summer the yucca produces a tall stalk of large, white flowers. You'll find the **narrow-leaf yucca** at Bryce Canyon, and the **Datil** (broad-leaf) and **Utah** varieties at Zion.

FLOWERING PLANTS

CLARET CUP CACTUS One of 14 varieties of cactus found in the desert areas of Zion National Park, the claret cup boasts one of the park's most beautiful flowers and sometimes produces its brilliant red blooms in spring, sometimes as early as March. The cactus stem (the body) is gray-green, cylindrical, 3 to 4 inches across, and covered with long, sharp, curved spines. As plants mature, numerous stems may grow, and they are stunning when covered with flowers.

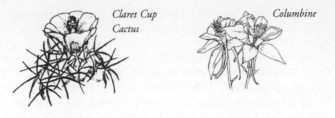

Claret Cup
Cactus

Columbine

COLUMBINE A member of the buttercup family, columbine come in a variety of intricate shapes and colors. Flowers have five petals, but the overall appearance can vary quite a bit. Columbine usually prefer shady, moist areas, such as Zion's hanging gardens, but will also grow in rocky canyons and open meadows. Species at Zion are the **golden columbine** (with a beautiful yellow flower) and the **western columbine** (with red and yellow flowers). In Bryce Canyon, you'll find **blue columbine** (the Colorado state flower) in meadows above 7,500 feet and in the high forest at the southern end of the park. Blooming season is late spring and early summer at Zion, and from mid- to late summer at Bryce Canyon.

LARKSPUR Another member of the buttercup family, the larkspur is represented by several families in the drier areas of both parks, blooming in summer. Flowers are small—about 1 inch across—and are blue, violet, or white.

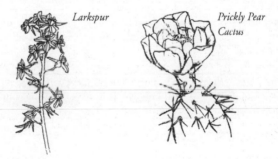

Larkspur

Prickly Pear
Cactus

PRICKLY PEAR CACTUS One of the easiest types of cactus to identify, as well as one of the most common, prickly pears have flattened paddle-shaped pads covered with spines. You'll find them throughout the drier areas of both parks, up to about 8,500 feet. Prickly pear usually bloom in late spring or early summer at Zion, a little later in Bryce Canyon, and produce pretty flowers, about 2 to

3 inches across. Flowers are mostly bright yellow, but sometimes pink or magenta. The plains and Englemann prickly pear you see at Zion are similar to the types usually encountered throughout the Southwest, with dull green pads and rigid spines an inch or so long. A bit unusual is the grizzly bear prickly pear that grows at Bryce Canyon. Although its pads are similar to other prickly pears, you can hardly see them because of what looks like long hair but is actually its spines, which are flexible, white, and sometimes up to a foot long.

SACRED DATURA   Dubbed the "Zion Lily" because of its abundance in the park, the sacred datura has large, funnel-shaped white flowers that open in the cool of night and are often closed by noon the next day. You'll see them frequently along roadsides and other areas where the soil has been disturbed, generally in dry, sandy soil below 7,000 feet elevation. Also called the Southwestern thorn apple, the sacred datura's flowers are 5 to 8 inches long and just as wide—the largest blossoms of any plant in southern Utah—and bloom from early spring to fall. Because it blossoms at night, it is also sometimes called the moon lily. *Warning:* The sacred datura is highly poisonous, and if any part of the plant is ingested it is likely to cause hallucinations, convulsions, and quite possibly death.

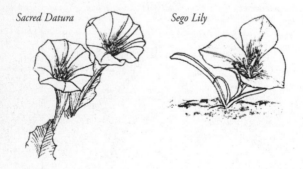

Sacred Datura   *Sego Lily*

SEGO LILY   Found in the drier areas below the rim in Bryce Canyon and in the canyons, cliffs, and plateaus of Zion, the sego lily has delicate white flowers, each about 1 to 2 inches wide. Flowers appear in late spring or early summer, and each is bell shaped, with three petals. The sego lily is the Utah state flower, and the state's early Mormon settlers ate the plant's bulbs when food was scarce.

4 The Fauna

Just as with these parks' plant life, elevation and availability of water determine what animals you'll see in any particular area. Zion, again, has the most diversity, with about 75 species of mammals, about 270 species of birds, and close to 30 species of reptiles and amphibians. Bryce Canyon also has plenty of wildlife to spot, though, with about 55 species of mammals, 160 species of birds, and about 15 species of reptiles and amphibians. Most of the animals in the lower elevations are those of the desert—small creatures such as lizards and snakes, kangaroo rats, rabbits, and squirrels. As the elevation increases, watch for prairie dogs, beavers, bighorn sheep, and mule deer. In the high forests of Bryce Canyon, keep an eye out for elk, pronghorn, and possibly black bear.

MAMMALS

BIGHORN SHEEP   Named for the large, curving horns on the rams, **desert bighorn sheep** are brown or light tan, with prominent white splotches on their rumps, faces, and legs. They inhabit isolated and harsh desert environments—what appear to be the most inhospitable areas. Your best chance to see bighorn sheep is in the steep, rocky areas on the east side of Zion National Park. They eat a variety of grasses and shrubs—practically whatever is available—and can go without water for more than 5 days.

Bighorn Sheep   *Black Bear*

BLACK BEARS   Although often black in the eastern United States, black bears in the West are usually brown or even tan. The males are big, up to about 6 feet tall and weighing over 500 pounds, but the females are much smaller. Bears like wooded areas, usually below 7,000 feet elevation, and there are occasional sightings in both parks. However, rather than actually seeing a bear in the flesh

✐ The Return of the Bighorn Sheep

Although there were reports of significant numbers of desert bighorns in the area now known as Zion National Park prior to the 20th century, the population gradually declined. This was due primarily to development of the land by settlers, who blocked access to water, planted crops, and brought in livestock that not only competed with the bighorns for grazing land but also introduced diseases. Another problem for the bighorns came with construction of the Zion–Mt. Carmel Highway and Tunnel in the 1920s, which effectively chopped their range in half. Park officials estimated that by the 1930s there were about 25 bighorns in the park and believe there were none left by the late 1950s.

Reintroduction efforts began in the mid-1960s, although it was not until 1973 that a dozen desert bighorns were captured in southern Nevada and brought to the park, where they were kept in an 80-acre enclosure. By 1976 there were 22 bighorns, still trapped in the enclosure, and park service wildlife biologists decided to release 13, moving them by helicopter to an isolated canyon in the southeastern corner of the park. Unfortunately, by the next year only 4 of the 13 had survived in the wild, due in part to the deaths of some by mountain lions, and this part of the reintroduction effort was considered a failure. By 1978, the population of the bighorns that remained in the enclosure had increased to 20, and they were released into the park. Although 9 died over the course of the next year, this release was considered a success.

Today there are at least 65 bighorns at Zion, and it appears that the herd is making a successful comeback, both in terms of reproduction and range expansion. Park officials believe the park could support at least twice as many desert bighorns, but at least for the time being there are no plans to introduce more from other areas, in part because of the fear that new animals would bring in new diseases.

(or the fur), it's more likely that you'll see signs of the bear's presence, such as decayed stumps or logs that have been torn apart for the grubs they contained, or tooth and claw marks on trees.

Interestingly, bear footprints look similar to those made by humans, with the addition of a small round mark above each toe produced by the bear's claws.

CHIPMUNKS Of the 22 species of chipmunks in North America, 21 can be found in the western United States. It is often difficult to tell one chipmunk species from another (at least for humans), but it's usually fairly easy to distinguish chipmunks from their cousins the squirrels, since chipmunks have black-and-white facial stripes while squirrels do not. Uinta, least, and cliff species of chipmunks will be found at both Bryce Canyon and Zion. The **cliff** chipmunk, which is often seen in rocky areas near cliffs, is usually the biggest of the three, sometimes reaching more than 10 inches long. The **Uinta** is usually seen scurrying about in pine and fir forests, such as those in both parks' campgrounds, while **least** chipmunks are at home in open areas of desert terrain, such as the beginning sections of the Under the Rim Trail at Bryce Canyon. All three have brown and gray fur, and black-and-white stripes on their backs (although the cliff chipmunks' stripes may be less distinct than the others), in addition to facial stripes.

Chipmunk   *Coyote*

COYOTES Survivors, coyotes are increasing in population throughout the United States. They are seen—or more often heard—throughout both Zion and Bryce Canyon, where they hunt rabbits, rodents, and other small animals. Tan or yellow-gray, with bushy tails, coyotes look much like domestic dogs and usually weigh 30 to 40 pounds. They can run at over 25 miles per hour, reaching 40 miles per hour for short periods. One way to easily distinguish between a dog and a coyote is that coyotes run with their tails down, while domestic dogs run with their tails up. Coyote choruses are often heard at night, consisting of a series of sharp yelps, barks, and howls.

ELK Although not believed to be full-time residents of either park, **Rocky Mountain elk** are known to be in the area and are sometimes spotted in or near the parks at the higher elevations, particularly in the fir and spruce forest at the southern end of Bryce Canyon National Park, and the Kolob Plateau in the northern part of Zion. Known for the buck's large racks of antlers, Rocky Mountain elk can reach weights of more than 1,000 pounds. Their coloring is usually brown or tan, with hints of yellow on their rumps and tails.

Elk

MOUNTAIN LIONS These large cats, usually solid tan or beige, are also known as panthers, cougars, and pumas. They are occasionally seen in both Bryce Canyon and Zion National Parks. However, there have been more sightings in Zion than in Bryce Canyon in recent years, and it is believed that there are quite a few in the backcountry areas of Kolob Canyon. At Bryce Canyon, you are most likely to see a mountain lion in the southern part of the park, in the backcountry along the Riggs Spring Loop Trail. Since they avoid humans, your best chance of seeing one is in a remote area or along a quiet roadway late at night. Skilled hunters, mountain lions prefer to catch deer, and a single mountain lion can kill and consume a mule deer a week if deer are plentiful. They also hunt coyotes, beavers, small mammals, and birds. Mountain lions will usually stash the leftovers from their kills, covering them with brush, sticks, and leaves, for later use.

MULE DEER The most commonly seen large animals at both parks, mule deer are often spotted near the campgrounds at Zion and along the Bryce Canyon scenic drive, especially in meadows along the edge of the forest. Considered medium-sized as deer go, mule deer are usually reddish brown in summer and gray during the winter, with patches of white on their rumps and throats year-round. However, their most distinguishing characteristic—what has given them their name—is their pair of huge, mulelike ears. Bucks can weigh up to about 450 pounds, while does usually weigh only about one-third of that.

Mountain Lion

Mule Deer

PRAIRIE DOG   These cute little critters are not dogs at all, but members of the squirrel family, making them rodents. The species at Bryce Canyon—the **Utah prairie dog**—is listed as a threatened species, which both amuses and annoys southern Utah ranchers, who consider it a pest. Utah prairie dogs are about a foot long, reddish-tan, and have small ears. Active during the day, prairie dogs live in park meadows in busy communities comprised of burrows, with mounds of dirt at each entrance. These colonies are strategically located in areas that have enough grass and other plants to sustain them, but with vegetation that is sparse and low enough for them to be able to spot predators with enough time to dart into their burrows. Prairie dogs seem to delight in alternately running about and standing at attention, making their antics popular with park visitors. *One warning, though:* The bacteria that causes bubonic plague has been found on fleas in prairie dog colonies in Bryce Canyon, so you should avoid getting too close. In any case, they bite.

PRONGHORN   Commonly seen in open fields in the vicinity of Bryce Canyon National Park—although not always within the park's boundaries—pronghorns were recently reintroduced into the area after being practically eliminated in the late 1800s and early 1900s. Sometimes called the American antelope, pronghorns are usually reddish-tan, with white on their rumps, chest, stomach, lower parts of their faces, and inner legs. Among the fastest animals in the world, pronghorns can reach speeds of 70 miles per hour, and their speed, combined with excellent eyesight, enable them to escape many of their predators.

Prairie Dog   *Pronghorn*

RABBITS   You'll probably see several species of rabbits while visiting Bryce Canyon and Zion National Parks. **Black-tailed jackrabbits,** easily recognized by their tall ears and black tails, are observed frequently along the cliffs at the rim of Bryce Canyon, and throughout Zion. Usually gaunt looking with mostly gray fur, they also have large hind feet. The cute **desert cottontails** are also found at both parks, although mostly at Zion in grasslands below 5,000 feet elevation. Desert cottontails are usually a brownish gray, with black-tipped ears and their trademark tail that looks just like a little white ball of cotton. Both species are favorite foods of the coyote.

Black-Tailed   *Desert*
Jackrabbit   *Cottontail*

RINGTAIL   Also known as miner's cats or ringtail cats, ringtails are not cats at all, but relatives of the raccoon. They have foxlike faces with big, round, dark eyes, but their most conspicuous feature is their long, bushy, black-and-white tail. The ringtail is usually about 30 inches long, and often more than half of that is tail.

Although common in Zion and present, although not in abundance, at Bryce Canyon, ringtails are seldom seen because they sleep all day in caves or other quiet places and emerge only after dark, when their super-sharp claws and catlike agility enable them to catch rodents, small mammals, birds, and insects. They are also not above raiding campsites. Ringtails got their nickname "miner's cats" because in the late 1800s and early 1900s they were taken into mines, where they quickly eliminated the mouse and rat populations.

Ringtail

SQUIRRELS   Practically every visitor to Zion and Bryce Canyon National Parks will see squirrels—at Zion, there's an abundance of **white-tailed antelope** and **rock** squirrels, while the most commonly seen species at Bryce Canyon is the **golden-mantled ground** squirrel, although there are plenty of rock and **red** squirrels as well. Often confused with chipmunks, which are generally the same size, shape, and coloring as squirrels, they are really quite easy to tell apart—chipmunks have stripes on the sides of their faces and squirrels do not. The golden mantled ground squirrel, which seems to think it owns the Bryce Canyon campgrounds, is especially attractive, with a white stripe bordered by two black stripes along each side of its brownish-gray body, and reddish-brown or copper-colored head and shoulders.

Squirrel

BIRDS

AMERICAN DIPPER   Also called water ouzels, these birds are seen year-round in the Narrows at Zion National Park, where they dive into the Virgin River in search of aquatic insects. Mostly slate-gray, with a stocky build, short tail, and wings, they run along the river bottom underwater, and in shallow areas appear to be water-skiing on the surface.

American Dipper

Mountain Chickadee

CHICKADEE   Mountain chickadees are abundant year-round at Bryce Canyon, both below the rim and throughout the ponderosa pine forest, up to 8,500 feet elevation; and in Zion in the piñon-juniper forest, such as along Watchman Trail, as well as the higher elevations. These small birds—only about 5 inches long—have pale, gray backs, jet-black caps and eye bands, and white cheeks, eye-brows, and chests.

Bald Eagle

Golden Eagle

EAGLES   Both **golden** and **bald** eagles are seen fairly frequently at Bryce Canyon, especially near the cliffs along the rim; and occa-sionally at Zion, where golden eagles are sometimes spotted in the canyons and on the plateaus, while bald eagles are more commonly seen near water, including the Virgin River and its tributaries. Both species are large, with wingspans usually over 6 feet. The golden

> **Fun Fact** **Eagle Not Regal**
>
> At least one of America's founding fathers was less than enthusiastic about selecting the bald eagle as the symbol of the country. In 1784 Benjamin Franklin wrote to his daughter Sarah, complaining that the bald eagle is "a bird of bad moral character," and stating, "The turkey is a much more respectable bird, and withal a true original native of America."

eagle is dark—brown and black—with a light gold color on the back of its neck. The bald eagle looks much like the golden eagle when young, but it develops a white head and tail and more solidly black body as it matures. Bald eagles have yellow bills, which are larger than the dark gray bills of golden eagles. While golden eagles eat rabbits and large rodents, bald eagles generally prefer fish, which is why they are usually seen near bodies of water. A few golden eagles are year-round residents of both parks; fall through spring is the best time to see bald eagles. (See also "Turkey Vulture," below.)

HERON   Large birds with long legs and necks, **great blue herons** are ideally suited for wading in the reservoirs and rivers in Zion National Park in search of a fish dinner. They will also eat insects, smaller birds, and rodents, and are sometimes seen as they migrate through the area in spring or fall. Great blue herons often stand over 4 feet tall, and have wingspans of almost 6 feet. In color, however, they are not really blue but mostly gray, with some black and white, and have a long, pointed yellow bill. Occasionally they are also seen in or near Bryce Canyon National Park.

Great Blue Heron

HUMMINGBIRDS These colorful little birds are delightful to watch, as they hover at flowers sipping nectar, perform rambunctious aerial mating dances, or warn other hummingbirds away with tail-fanning and other displays. (You might also notice that hummingbirds can fly backward—they're the only birds known to do this.) Among the species at Zion are the **black-chinned, Costa's, broad-tailed,** and **rufous;** while at Bryce Canyon, you will most likely see the black-chinned and broad-tailed, although rufous are occasionally spotted. The most colorful among these are the rufous: The males are a startling reddish-brown with an iridescent red-orange throat, while females have green backs with areas of reddish-brown on their tails and flanks.

Black-Chinned Hummingbird

Broad-Tailed Hummingbird

JAYS Among the noisiest and most raucous-sounding birds, jays are almost always heard before they are seen, although because of their size—sometimes a foot long—these year-round residents of both parks are easy to spot as well. **Scrub jays,** seen at numerous locations at both Zion and Bryce Canyon, often have a brilliant blue back, white or gray underneath, and a black mask. **Steller's jays** are bright blue on their lower half and flat black above, with a prominent crest on the top of their heads. **Piñon jays** are a deep blue almost all over, with a bit of white on their throats and possibly other markings.

Scrub Jay

Steller's Jay

Piñon Jay

Pygmy Nuthatch

NUTHATCHES Seen year-round throughout both Bryce Canyon and Zion, especially at higher elevations, nuthatches are known for their ability to walk down tree trunks with their heads aimed straight down. The **white-breasted** nuthatch is the species most commonly spotted at Zion, sometimes along the upper sections of the West Rim Trail or in the Kolob Canyon area; it's also seen in various locations throughout Bryce Canyon. A white-breasted nuthatch is about 6 inches long, with a blue back; a white face, chest, and belly; and a black cap on its head. The **pygmy** nuthatch is commonly seen in the ponderosa pine forests in Bryce and occasionally observed in Zion. This tiny bird, rarely more than 4½ inches from the tip of its beak to the tip of its tail, is bluish-gray on its back and sides, white or light gray underneath, and it has a dark cap on its head. Also frequently seen at Bryce Canyon—generally in the forests above 8,500 feet—but only occasionally at Zion are **red-breasted** nuthatches, which, not surprisingly, are recognized by their red or rust-colored chests. They have blue-gray backs and dark crowns, plus white eyebrows and a dark line behind each eye.

PEREGRINE FALCON Fairly common along the cliffs just below the rim at Bryce Canyon, and occasionally seen at Zion, peregrine falcons have wingspans that often exceed 3 feet, which helps make them one of the world's fastest birds, able to exceed 200 miles per hour. They're known to breed at Zion and sometimes nest in the Weeping Rock area. Their back and wings are usually slate-gray or blue-gray, which also projects vertically down their face in bands over their eyes. The rest of their face and neck is a light gray or white, and underneath these falcons are usually a medium gray. During peregrine falcon nesting, which takes place from early spring to July, some areas at Zion National Park are off-limits to rock climbers. Pesticides drastically reduced the number of peregrine

---

Tips **Tip for Wildlife Watchers**

Although it's generally true that you'll see most animals—especially mammals—early and late in the day, finding a quiet spot can be almost as important. For instance, you're likely to see **mule deer** in Watchman Campground at Zion in midday. When practically all the campers have left for the trails or scenic drives, the deer take advantage of the quiet to stop in for a drink in the creek.

---

falcons in the United States in the 1950s and 1960s, and by 1970 there were only 39 breeding pairs known to exist in the continental United States. But after years on the endangered species list they are on the increase again, thanks to a ban on many pesticides, and in 1999 there were sufficient numbers of the birds that they were removed from the list. Interestingly, you'll also see peregrines in cities, where they nest on tall buildings or bridges and dine on pigeons.

Peregrine Falcon   *Red-Tailed Hawk*

RED-TAILED HAWK Year-round residents of both Bryce Canyon and Zion, red-tailed hawks are always on the lookout for small rodents, the mainstay of their diet. They're often seen as they glide over open areas in search of prey—watch for them over the hoodoos in Bryce Canyon—or perch in a tree at the edge of a meadow, watching for any movement in the grass. Stocky, with wingspans of about 4 feet, red-tails are named for their rust-colored tails. Their chests and faces are usually white, and their upper parts are variable, from light to dark brown.

SWALLOWS   Known for their long, pointed wings and superb grace while flying, flocks of swallows are often seen in both parks during the summer, soaring over the meadows and plateaus, and along the cliffs at the rim of Bryce Canyon. The most commonly seen species are **violet-green** swallows—pretty little birds with striking, metallic-green backs, bright violet on their tails, and white faces and lower parts. Also watch for **cliff** swallows in both parks, not only near cliffs but also in the woods along the Virgin River at Zion. Cliff swallows have mostly blue-gray upper parts, with white below, but also often have dark auburn throats and foreheads.

Violet-Green Swallow

Cliff Swallow

SWIFTS   This speedy bird (thus the name) not only catches and consumes its dinner of insects while flying, but also never perches, clinging instead to trees and other vertical surfaces. **White-throated** swifts are found during the summer in the canyons and cliffs at both Zion and Bryce Canyon, often in the same areas as violet-green swallows. White-throated swifts are basically black and white—the wings, tail, and top of the head are black, the lower face, throat, and most of the chest are white.

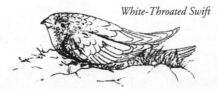

White-Throated Swift

TURKEY VULTURE   Bird-watchers in both Zion and Bryce Canyon have reported sightings of turkey vultures, also called buzzards, which are about the same size as eagles and, when flying, are sometimes mistaken for golden eagles. The main visual difference is that the turkey vulture has a red head, and unlike the golden eagle it can glide seemingly forever without flapping its wings, riding on columns of warm air known as thermals.

Turkey Vulture

REPTILES & AMPHIBIANS
CANYON TREE FROG   Often camouflaged among rocks near pools and streams in Zion National Park's side canyons, the canyon tree frog is generally olive, gray, or brown with indistinct dark patches on its back. From 1¼ to 2¼ inches long, it often has a light spot below its eye. During the spring mating season, you can often hear a lively chorus of tree frogs.

Canyon
Tree Frog   *Rattlesnake*

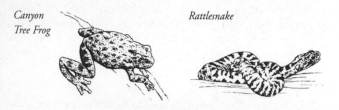

GREAT BASIN RATTLESNAKE   A subspecies of the western rattlesnake, the Great Basin rattlesnake is found both above and below the rim at Bryce Canyon, and in most areas of Zion. Generally they hibernate in winter, so you will most likely encounter them only April through October. Sometimes growing to more than 5 feet long, they are usually gray or light brown with dark patches on their backs. They have wide, triangular-shaped flat heads, and bony, interlocking segments on their tails, which produce a buzzing or hissing noise when shaken—this usually happens when the snake is agitated. Each time the snake sheds its skin, which can occur up to five times a year, the rattle gets a new segment. These snakes are highly poisonous, but usually only attack humans when they feel threatened. Because they are mainly nocturnal, those walking in isolated areas at night should use flashlights to avoid stepping on them.

MOUNTAIN SHORT-HORNED LIZARD These little lizards—usually between 2 and 4 inches long—are found in abundance in a variety of habitats in Bryce Canyon National Park and at higher elevations at Zion. They are active mostly during the day, and their diet consists mainly of ants, but they will also eat other insects and even small snakes. Mountain short-horned lizards have a broad, flat body, short tail, and short horns on the back of their heads. They are usually a reddish brown, with darker spots on their backs.

Short-Horned Lizard

NORTHERN SAGEBRUSH LIZARD Commonly seen on trails below the rim at Bryce Canyon National Park and in the dry, open areas of rocks and sagebrush at Zion, the northern sagebrush lizard is slim, at least compared to the mountain short-horned lizard discussed above, and brown to grayish green in color; the males have blue markings on their bellies. This lizard may also have stripes of various shades of brown or light tan running the length of its body.

INVERTEBRATES

ZION SNAIL One creature unique to Zion National Park is the Zion snail, which you'll only find clinging to wet canyon walls in a 4-mile section of the Narrows along the Virgin River—the Riverside Walk as it enters the Narrows is a good place to see them. The walls are kept moist by seeps and springs, which also nurture hanging gardens. This tiny snail, complete with shell, is a mere ⅛ inch or less across, and to the naked eye appears to be just a dark brown or black speck on a shiny, wet wall. They hold on to the slick walls with a suction-cup foot, which in proportion to the creature's size is the biggest foot of any snail, a phenomenon that has caused some park rangers to refer to the Zion snail as "our little bigfoot." Please do not attempt to touch these fragile creatures.

5 The Ecosystem

So far, Zion and Bryce Canyon National Parks have managed to escape most of the serious ecological problems that plague some of America's other national parks, such as air and water pollution from nearby cities, adjacent mining, and extreme overcrowding (with its resultant air and noise pollution from automobiles). Still, there is the threat of air pollution from power plants across the Colorado Plateau, and the park service has additional concerns over how Bryce Canyon and Zion National Parks can be best managed to both preserve their often delicate ecosystems and produce a rewarding experience for park visitors.

Presently, visitors to both Zion and Bryce Canyon can still get away from humanity fairly easily by heading out onto park trails or into the backcountry, and they can still find relatively unspoiled areas there. To preserve these unspoiled areas and their ecosystems, increasing efforts are being made in both parks to make visitors understand the need for zero-impact visitation, or as close as people can get to that short of staying home. In most cases, people are getting the message and are doing their best to stay on trails, not pollute water or drop trash, and certainly not to disturb the parks' plants and animals. In addition, shuttle bus systems have been implemented at both parks to help relieve traffic congestion and parking problems.

One issue that is expected to take on more importance in the years to come—and over which the National Park Service has little control—is increasing development in nearby communities. Major hotels have recently been built in Springdale, just outside Zion; and some degradation to Bryce Canyon's delightful night sky is feared from continuing development just outside that park's entrance.

Meanwhile, within park boundaries the main issue—both now and for the future—is overcrowding, and how it affects the variety of habitats that support a vast array of plant and animal life. Officials of the National Park Service have taken the position that they do not want to limit the number of people who visit the parks, and in late 1997, Department of the Interior Secretary Bruce Babbitt said, "The problem isn't too many people, it's too many cars." Babbitt was talking about the planned ban on private motor vehicles at Zion, plus similar plans at Grand Canyon and Yosemite National Parks. Added Rodney Slater, Secretary of Transportation, "It's time for us to build a transit system for the 21st century that allows us to spend more time sighting bears than looking for a parking spot."

This issue of how the parks can handle an increasing number of visitors brings to mind the question of the entire philosophy of the National Park Service, which essentially is to accomplish two goals simultaneously—preserve resources and promote visitor enjoyment. But which is more important: protecting the plants, animals, and geologic formations that make these parks the special places they are, or helping people enjoy these very same plants, animals, and geologic formations?

In an interview with the nonprofit **National Parks and Conservation Association,** published in the November/December 1997 issue of the association's magazine, *National Parks,* National Park Service Director Robert Stanton said that resource protection should take precedence over the public's enjoyment. But he added, "It is a management decision to discern what level of visitor use can be accommodated without harming in an irreparable way the resources. . . . It's an easy thing to describe; it's a difficult thing to accomplish."

Essentially, the question is how far should parks go to accommodate their visitors—the people who pay the entrance and user fees and in most cases the tax dollars that fund the parks—and at what point does each and every visitor's impact become unacceptable? It's a tightrope for park managers and a debate both within and outside the park service that will not be settled soon, if ever.

Index

See also Accommodations and Restaurant indexes below.

ACCOMMODATIONS

RESTAURANTS